Catapult Your Business to New Heights

CATAPULT YOUR BUSINESS TO NEW HEIGHTS

Sure-Fire Strategies to Increase Profit

Glory Borgeson

PINNACLE
PUBLICATIONS, INC.

Pinnacle Publications, Inc.
P. O. Box 4224
Wheaton, IL 60189

Design: Wayne E. Johnson
wayneej@comcast.net

Quotations included at the beginning of each chapter were obtained from the following Web sites:
    www.elibron.com
    http://quotations.about.com
    www.worldofquotes.com
    www.dictionaryquotes.com
    www.brainyquote.com
    www.enotes.com
    www.quotecosmos.com

ISBN: 978-0-9820507-3-6

First printing 2009

Printed in the United States of America

10 9 8 7 6 5 4 3 2 1

Table of Contents

Disclaimer

*T*his book is designed to provide information about running a small business. It is sold with the understanding that the publisher and author are not engaged in rendering legal or accounting services. If legal assistance is required, the services of a competent professional should be sought.

The purpose of this book is to educate and inform. The author and Pinnacle Publications, Inc. shall have neither liability nor responsibility to any person or entity with respect to any loss or damage caused, or alleged to have been caused, directly or indirectly, by the information contained in this book.

Acknowledgments

*P*eople have told me for years that they love to receive gifts from me, from the actual gift I choose right down to the exquisite packaging. Writing and publishing a book is a lot like preparing a gift for a special person. I start with ideas, take time to select the right words to express those ideas, and package them exquisitely—hoping that reading the book will bring you happiness, wealth, and wisdom.

Likewise, creating a book involves receiving gifts *from* people that involve their time, energy, and input to make my "book dream" a reality.

I'd like to thank the people who read the first manuscript, who then gave me many ideas for making the book better: Lauren Evans DeJong, Michelle Eppley, and Tom Canale.

Next, I'd like to give a big thank you to people I met several years ago at the National Speakers Association—Illinois Chapter, who spent time with me, encouraged me in my book endeavor, gave me ideas and resources, let me pull knowledge out of their brains, and allowed me to e-mail them, call them, and meet with them to share their vast stores of wisdom with me: Al Lautenslager, Conor Cunneen, Deb DiSandro, Rita Emmett, and Harry Dubnick.

Every author appreciates an endorsement, and I am no exception. I'd like to thank the endorsers of *Catapult*: Jay Conrad Levinson, Barry Moltz, Susan Harrow, Al Lautenslager, and Curt Coffman. You all helped me understand the power of an endorsement.

Acknowledgments _____

The people who encouraged me to write, and to write well, deserve special acknowledgement. From my "student years," Linda Rhodes, my 8th grade English teacher, who taught me to appreciate the written and spoken English word (with some humor added in for good measure!); and Dr. Roald Tweet, my first writing instructor at Augustana College, who did an incredible job instilling good research and writing techniques in his students, as only masterful teachers can do with a roomful of freshman. Two other people who encouraged me to write well (this time for money) came along in my life during one of the times that I changed my career. Getting paid to write as an instructional designer gave me the tools and experience I needed to move me toward other types of writing. Thanks to Christine Abbott, who taught me a lot about writing in order to teach adults so that they can really absorb the material and apply it appropriately; and thanks to Jacqueline Napier, who led me to Christine and to many other resources that have made good writing possible.

Pull a Rabbit Out of a Hat

"Business must be profitable if it is to continue to succeed, but the glory of business is to make it so successful that it may do things that are great chiefly because they ought to be done."

—Charles M. Schwab

*O*wning a business—calling your own shots, writing your own rules, setting your own hours, giving yourself a raise—this is the dream of many people, not just in this country but all over the world. We envision making a six-figure salary every year (at least!) and carving out our own destinies. We assure ourselves that other people's ideas, goals, and agendas will no longer get in our way. Finally—*finally*—we won't have to dance to the boss's tune; we will set our own hours and have the free time to spend with our families. Or we'll improve our golf game. Or we'll swim, or paint, or have lunch with friends on a weekday, or take a break in Jamaica during the on-season for once instead of waiting our turn with the rest of the employees to sign up for vacation time.

Millions of people have already made the switch to being self-employed. If you are reading this book, perhaps you are one of the millions of entrepreneurs of this world who have sought the freedom and the responsibility of running your own business. If so, then you are familiar with the difficulties that are involved, the problems you never anticipated when you were busy dreaming about all that freedom. The reality of managing everything yourself is that you lie awake at night trying to deal with the stress that accompanies entrepreneurship. You wonder if you will ever see the day when you actually make the kind of profit you hoped for. You wish you could stop and take a vacation anytime, let alone the very week you want one.

Is it possible to make a success of your business without allowing stress to take over? Can you really increase profitability, yet also reduce the strain of all the responsibility? *Or is that like asking someone to pull a rabbit out of a hat?*

"It's a nice trick," you think, "but it can't be done." In this book, you will learn that you can pull a rabbit out of a hat. You can catapult your business to a greater level of profit without losing your mind. As you will see, most entrepreneurs make the same kinds of mistakes:

- They don't outsource enough tasks.
- They underestimate how much cash they'll need to get their company off the ground.
- They have no idea how hard it will be on the relationship if they decide to work with their spouse.
- If they choose to work out of their home instead of operating out of an office, they can't figure out how to keep workspace separate from living space; work takes over life.
- They have difficulty managing their own invoicing, bill-paying, or other accounting functions.
- They don't delegate enough tasks to others in order to leave themselves free to attend to more important activities.

- They keep letting work time seep into playtime.
- They haven't figured out how to rent or lease office space.
- They don't add and refine the entrepreneurial skills they are lacking.

Every one of these is a challenge, but they don't have to drive you crazy. All you have to do is learn how to handle the tasks. This book is about teaching yourself how to have the best of both worlds: You can learn to take on the challenges *and* make a healthy profit *and* not make yourself sick from stress.

Are You as Tired as I Am?

Most business owners started out by working for someone else earlier in their careers. This is how they learned the ropes. Of course, when somebody else signs your paycheck, that person has a number of expectations of you in return, and the one that looms largest is how many hours a week he expects you to work. If you were in this trap, you probably thought, "When I escape this asylum, I'll be home for the six o'clock news every night. I'll put my kids to bed myself." What you didn't realize is that you were being conditioned to think that 50- and 60-hour work weeks ought to be the norm. The idea crept into your mind that anything less than that meant you were goofing off. Today, as your own boss, you are no easier on yourself than your old boss used to be. Working for yourself has not provided the freedom you thought it would. You look around and what do you see? All your competitors are working 50 to 60 hours a week. You have to do the same—don't you?

Unfortunately, that really is the mentality of the business world today. Thirty years ago, a normal work week was 40 hours. If somebody wanted you to put in more time, it was a rarity; people put in overtime only to finish a particular project. Perhaps they did it once or twice a year at the most. Today, employers routinely expect their people to work more than forty hours a week and nobody even blinks.

Even though business owners are technically free to ignore this trend since they are in charge of themselves, they inevitably fall prey to this phenomenon. They pressure themselves to work longer hours out of a fear that if they don't, they'll fall behind. This is our *Zeitgeist*, the spirit of this age. However, it is very hard to reconcile this mentality with a relaxed, balanced life. Remember the old saying? "All work and no play makes Jack a dull boy." Well, nowadays, it also makes Jack a sick boy. Jack is up against a system that is working him to death—literally. The Japanese have a word for death from overwork: It's called *Karoshi*. This means that the phenomenon of work/stress related death is so common in Japan, they actually have coined a single word for it. And it must be spreading because the *Oxford English Dictionary Online* now contains that word as well.

As far as I know, however, the Japanese have not yet coined a word for work/stress *illness*, which affects a far larger number of people and is harder to track. Workers are treated for heart attacks, hypertension, strokes, depression, and more. Does anyone ask if these are related to tension on the job? If somebody gets in a car accident because he is so distracted by anxiety that he's not paying attention to the road, does anybody wonder if it occurred because he was overagitated by a deadline he won't meet for a client? At least the Japanese have come to recognize other problems, for instance, suicide-by-overwork: It is called *karojisatsu*.

On June 13, 2004, the *Chicago Tribune* reported that the Japanese are also noticing a rising incidence of sleep disorders. Remarkably, these start as early in life as elementary school when the little students have to stay up late studying. Thus, they begin a lifelong habit of working too hard and making their health suffer for it. In adulthood, the trend merely continues. Homework is replaced by take-home tasks and school is replaced by the workplace. And of course, for adults one has to add in the tension they suffer from sitting in stand-still traffic to commute long distances to the job. In the year 2000, Japan's Health Ministry reported that 31 percent of their people said they didn't get enough sleep because of work, school, or commuting. Another 29 percent attributed their lack of sleep directly to stress.

To alleviate this problem, you would think that their society might say: "Let's not work so much. We'll all have better lives." Instead, they thought they could eliminate the problem by designing a "sleep machine," which sells for about $30,000. It is a combination of a very fancy chair, a large screen TV, and a sound system to play music. The manufacturer, Matushita Electric Works, claims that it gives its users a full eight hours of peaceful sleep (apparently no matter what condition in their lives created the sleeplessness in the first place). Can't afford this little contraption in the home? Easily fixed. Japanese companies have purchased the system for their overworked employees and set it up in a special room amidst the offices. People can use it during the day to get a little shut eye.

Companies in North America, likewise, have recognized the need to reduce stress in the workplace. Some have created "fun rooms" or "creativity rooms." These spaces are equipped with couches, bean bag chairs, foosball tables, televisions, stereos, and stocked refrigerators. They look something like a recreational room in a college dorm.

The companies who install them, however, are ignoring a fundamental paradox: For employees to benefit from fun rooms, they have to actually *use* them. A couple of years ago, I was visiting a client at a company that had one of these adult rec rooms. Every time I walked past it, it was empty. I always knew I could use the phone in that room with complete privacy because I was the only person there. No one else could pry herself away from her desk long enough to drop by and relax.

Who is the corporate world kidding? These are Band-aid solutions to surgical-size wounds, a stop-gap measure for a serious situation. But what if you could find a real solution? Believe it or not, you can get all your work done, be on the job only 40 hours a week, and still make a very healthy profit.

Are We Having Fun Yet?

Common wisdom tells us that with a 40-hour work week (minus vacations and holidays), we are spending about 1,960 hours a year on the job. Over a period of 50 years (from age 21 to age 70), that adds up to 98,000 hours of work. Sound like a lot? Well, don't worry, there are 306,600 hours left over for sleep and play. This works out to about 5,890 hours of free time every year. Do you feel like you spend that many hours a year taking it easy? More than 5000 hours!

This exercise reminds me of something a college roommate told me years ago, an incident in which her German teacher claimed that his 24-hour days were divided up into equal thirds, with eight hours of sleep, eight of play, and eight of work. If that were true, he would comfortably fall into the statistics listed above. When she told me this, however, I thought, "He can't be serious. I'm only a student and I get less than eight hours sleep a night. And I know that a third of my day isn't spent having fun. So the rest of the time must be spent on *work*."

Think about everything you do outside your business day. You cook, clean, do the laundry, pay bills, run errands, commute, and chauffeur the kids. That's not play; it's unpaid work, in addition to the time you spend in the office. Even if you have a civilized job that only demands 40 hours a week, you are still spending about 66 percent of your time remaining on the other types of "work" you have to do. That leaves you with a meager 2 percent of your day for recreation. By my calculation, that comes out to 122.6 hours a year or a little more than 20 minutes a day. In that time you can, let's see...play with the dog, kick the cat, interrogate your teenager, and compulsively switch channels on the TV set.

This book cannot solve the conundrum of what to do about the lack of recreational time in modern life. What I can point out is that this is all the more reason to pay attention to the quality of the time you *do* spend at your business because it takes up such a large chunk of your life. Work is not time-out. It is an essential part of your life, and it matters whether it is satisfying, relaxing, and meaningful, or whether you feel no better off than an indentured serf. If we only worked 10 minutes a day, this would not be an issue; we can put up with anything for 10 minutes. But our job occupies the largest mass of time spent at a single activity, so it matters a great deal how we run our business. What is the level of our quality of life while we're at work? We hear it all the time that we work to support a certain lifestyle, but lifestyle is the whole package: the home, the vacation, the family—*and* the job or business. Make sure you look at your life as a whole.

The trends in the go-go-go business world make me want to rebel. I would, in fact, like to revolutionize the way we do business. I don't want the ways of the world to dictate a stressed-out existence in which I can only hope to break even financially. In reality, it is possible to make a good profit *and* enjoy my life—not have to choose between the two.

My solution is to transform how we work so that we are very productive, earn a solid income, yet clock no more than 40 hours a week at our business. Running your own business shouldn't be more time-consuming or more of a burden than punching in for somebody else's company.

To catapult your profits into the stratosphere without losing your mind, you first need to assess what the equation looks like to you. In basic business-and-life language, to "increase profit and decrease stress" means different things to different people. For example, it might mean that:

- "I am working 40 hours a week or less, and my income is at least $150,000."
- "Our business grosses $700,000, nets $300,000, and we have time to go to our kids' softball games and karate practice."

- "My business supports my family, funds my retirement plan, pays my employees, and allows me the time off that I need."
- "I make enough money to have a comfortable lifestyle that doesn't cause high blood pressure."

As you can see from the list above, most people want two things out of running their business: increased profit and decreased stress. They believe, however, that one must always give way to the other. For example, if they pursue a lifestyle where they have plenty of free time and their mind isn't taken over by concerns with their company, then they wonder if their company will end up with the short end of the stick. They won't be giving it the time, energy, or attention it deserves, and it will fail to thrive. It won't provide enough income for the desired carefree lifestyle. On the other hand, if they make the business their top priority, then they wonder if it will consume them and dominate their life —plenty of money but no life to speak of outside of work. So it seems as if they can't have both, that one cancels the other. *"If I want plenty of money, I have to spend the time to make it, which will drain time from the rest of my life."*

This is a myth. You *can* have both. The secret is to transform your style of doing business so that it works for you and for your life. You have to change how you, as the owner, run your enterprise so that it causes less stress to deal with the challenges of being a business owner in today's world, yet you stay on top of profit. In short, you will learn that

9

by running your business as a *well-oiled machine*, you can increase your profit *and* decrease your stress at the same time.

Stress

Why do I keep emphasizing the issue of decreasing stress? In the traditional definitions of success, all they talk about is how much money you make. They don't seem concerned with how you feel (with your quality of life, in other words) while you're making that money. Money itself can't buy happiness. That's the oldest slogan in the book, but it bears repeating because we are so easily seduced into thinking that it can. After all, this is the very thinking that fuels a consumer economy. How much good is a fat bank account if you're miserable or unhealthy?

My father is a case in point. He owned a small manufacturing company in Chicago when I was growing up. The income he produced supported a very decent lifestyle for him and his family. We grew up in a spacious house, took exciting family vacations every year, and we all went to college. Even though he didn't put in a lot of overtime by today's standards, he still drove himself crazy on the job and all that tension built up in his body. At age 53, he had a stroke from the stress and died four years later.

I have met many entrepreneurs over the years, and I have come to one conclusion about all of them: It is no benefit at all to make a handsome profit if you are too stressed to enjoy it. So you've got a lot of money in the bank. If you die young, you won't be around to spend it. Is that your goal—to die young and leave a hefty inheritance?

As a business owner myself, I decided several years ago that I shouldn't have to make the choice between money and health, or money and happiness, or money and tranquility. This might sound entitled, but I didn't see why I couldn't have it all. The conclusion I came to, when I really began to observe how I and my counterparts ran our businesses, was that the companies weren't driving us crazy; *we were driving ourselves crazy.*

- We weren't working or managing in ways that were efficient and productive.
- We weren't using our time well.
- We weren't putting the money we reinvested to good use.
- We had plenty of bad habits that sabotaged all our best efforts.
- We weren't developing the right skills.

I have known plenty of people who ran profitable businesses, but their stress levels were off the charts. The only way they could manage their success rate was to work 60- to 80-hour weeks, and in the time left over they worried about all the tasks left unfinished that day. They didn't sleep well at night. They ate too much and had too many three-martini lunches. They were overweight, had nervous skin conditions, or developed chronic aches and pains. In the worst cases, they had heart attacks and strokes, or they got cancer. (Yes, cancer has been linked to stress.) In every case, the inner tension was written all over their faces. People who were 40 years old looked as if they were close to retirement age.

And if it wasn't their health that took the worst hit, it was their family life. They had kids who were acting out as teenagers because one or both working parents were largely absent from their childhoods. If their marriages held together, it was by a thread. All their close relationships occurred through work. In short, their companies were eating up their lives.

This is not right.

When I tell you that you can decrease your stress, it doesn't mean I'm going to give you a list of ways to relax. I'm not specifically going to advocate getting two massages a week (although it can't hurt), or doing yoga between business meetings, or applying the power of positive thinking.

What I am talking about, simply, is making your business work better so you don't have to work harder. In engineering, there is a word that means using the least amount of effort to produce the greatest results; it's called *leverage*. This is what I am encouraging you to do. Learn to run your business so efficiently that no matter how many difficulties rise up, you are in a position to handle them efficiently and easily with the least amount of effort and time.

Transforming the way you work will decrease your stress in several ways:

- It will give you more time for relaxing recreational activities.
- It will give you the peace of mind of knowing that your company is running like a well-oiled machine.
- You will become better organized, erasing the clutter from your mind and from your office.
- It will release you from worrying about your business when you are with family and friends, thus strengthening your relationships.

- You will have more money to spend so you won't have to be anxious about your financial future.

Just as you go to the gym to get your body in shape, so you need to "work out" with the ideas and information in this book to get your company in shape. Think of this book as your own personal trainer or coach, right by your side offering guidance, encouragement, and advice. I am going to put you through the right exercises to train you as an expert entrepreneur so that you and your business are tough, buff, and ready to compete. The key is to achieve the right balance that allows you to make a great income without sacrificing your mind and body. This takes discipline, but the payoff is well worth your while.

When you apply these principles to your own company and to yourself as its leader, you will find yourself in great "profit-shape." The stress will melt away like giant icicles in the sun. Bit by bit, the icicles that have weighed you down in the past will disappear and your business will be transformed.

What's It All About?

By reading and working through *Catapult Your Business to New Heights*, you will transform your business and your life. You will begin by developing a vision for both your business and your personal life that helps you create and sustain an ongoing venture that provides for your customers over the long-term, and helps you create a life that you want.

Creating a strategy is the next important phase. Do you ever get bogged down with urgent tasks that take you away from the more important responsibilities you need to do? Is it hurting your profitability? This book will help you work on prioritizing, focusing, and changing your schedule and your thinking in order to make more space in your life, which will significantly reduce your stress. Focusing your time on what's important will also lead to increased profit.

To keep a business going for the long-term (and profitably), it's crucial to set up your business' structure and systems in such a way that they can eventually run while you're absent. Doesn't that sound like a good idea? You can actually get away from your business and it keeps running well. You make money even when you're on vacation! Just like your body needs a skeleton and skin to hold its structure, so does your business need a structure to hold it together. And just like your body needs a circulatory system, nervous system, and digestive system in order to live, your business needs various types of systems (including communications, sales, purchasing, and fulfillment systems) to keep it alive and well.

Your customers are your lifeblood. To become a business that's known for its great customer service, you will learn how to develop your customers into *loyal* customers who not only return to buy again, but who also tell others great news about you.

To further decrease your stress and increase your profit, you'll learn about the difference between delegation and duplication, why they are both important to your business, and how to leverage them to your benefit. By doing so, you'll have more time to lead a great team with your employees and to develop non-employee teams that help you become more successful.

If customers are the lifeblood of your business, then sales and marketing are the tools that attract them and pump that lifeblood through the business. Building up your sales skills and marketing strategies helps you to become more visionary as you flex creative muscles and develop new ideas. Naturally, increasing sales increases your profit, while developing plans and systems to generate sales decreases your stress.

When your financial house is in order, you sleep better at night, right? Knowing how to handle your finances, how to interpret financial statements, and when to delegate financial responsibilities is part of handling your finances with finesse. You will learn about financial issues so as to interpret your increasing profitability and get those extra "zzz's".

The whole idea of catapulting your business to new (profitable) heights and decreasing stress is to live a balanced life with time and resources for the people and activities you enjoy. After you have worked through most of this book and learned about getting your business in shape for greater profitability, you will learn about ways to further decrease the stress in your life.

To make reading this book an even more worthwhile exercise, I suggest you purchase a spiral notebook and use it as a journal. As you read, write your thoughts into the journal, and then use the *Application section* at the end of each chapter to apply the principles of the chapter to your own business.

Is this Book for You?

This book is right for you if you fall into one of the following categories:

- You own a business and have fewer than 500 employees.
- You own a business and you have no employees (you are a "solopreneur").

- You want to own a business some day, and when you do, you would like it to be a success financially and personally.

This book is for you if you are like me—*you want to have the best of both worlds*. You want *great profits* as well as the *peace of mind* to enjoy them. Read on!

Develop Your Vision

*"Vision without action is a daydream. Action
without vision is a nightmare."*

—Japanese Proverb

A friend of mine, Phil, once pointed out a beautiful house built close to where he worked. He remembered when the land was empty. He recalled meeting the architect who was in the process of designing the home shortly after the vacant land was purchased by a developer. The architect and Phil were outside next to the property and talking about the plans for the property. The architect explained to Phil in great detail how the 3000 square foot house would look, how it would be situated to take advantage of the views, and how the landscaping would enhance the outer visual appeal of the house. For the life of him, Phil just could not envision the house and the landscaping even close to how it turned out. He could picture a *house* there, but just not the house the architect had in mind.

The architect, however, had a very specific vision in his mind for how this house would look. He knew it would definitely grab the attention of anyone driving by—not because it was gaudy, but because it was spectacular and tasteful. Once the home was complete and the landscaping was finished, Phil agreed it was a well-designed piece of work. He also admired the talent of the architect to be able to envision this gorgeous home, placed properly on the land, one year earlier when all that was there was vacant property.

A vision is a picture in your mind of something that you want to happen in the future. By "future," that can mean six months, 20 years, or any amount of time in between. It may include only a few details or many details. A vision is something like a dream, but it is more real than a dream; first, because you want it to happen, and second, because you will take action to make it happen.

Catapulting your business to new heights starts out with a vision. You get a picture in your mind about what you want for your business and for your life. For some people, envisioning this becomes more than just a picture; it becomes an actual feeling. Perhaps it becomes a feeling of freedom, joy, excitement, relief, or gratitude.

Whatever the vision, dream, or feeling, increasing your profit and decreasing your stress is a difficult task. If it was easy to accomplish, every business owner would already be there. But it is not easy and many never get there. Some achieve one but do not achieve the other. Some entrepreneurs spend too many years with high stress and low profits before they finally get to high profits and low stress.

In this chapter you will start to carve out your vision. Use your journal to record your thoughts and impressions and use the Application section at the end of the chapter to really focus on your business. Refer to your notes frequently as you read the book. Add more notes to your vision as ideas come to you.

It is a good idea to revisit your vision for your business and personal life annually. Circumstances change and priorities occasionally change, too. Keep your notes handy so that you can revise your vision as needed.

A Vision is Created to Work for You

Whether you have already achieved a great or small amount of success, or are just starting out, you may or may not have already developed a vision for your business and your life. Many people who become successful actually wrote out what they wanted to achieve (and when they wanted to achieve it) some years prior to achieving that success. Other successful people may not be able to point to a time when they wrote out their vision and their goals. However, most likely at some point in time they pictured in their minds what they wanted, when they wanted it, and how they would go about achieving it, even if they did not actually write it down. When you take some time to purposely think through your dreams and write them out, your action puts motion and life into your dreams. You can actually motivate yourself with the words you write.

What are the benefits *to you* of creating a vision for your business and your life? There are several, and they directly affect the outcome of your business.

Your vision for your business (and for you as its owner) gets you thinking in terms of expansion, growth, and the future. A vision is all about the future. It involves picturing in your mind's eye various details about the business, its size, and the money it makes. When you get your thoughts set on a vision for your business, and then go back to review your vision time after time, you get your mind exercised in terms of forthcoming expansion and profit.

Over time, a vision will help you stay focused. For example, when a manufacturing entrepreneur loses a big account and could be dragged down about it, reviewing his vision can give him back the spark that he needs to get his sight back on his goals. Likewise, in the future, when things are not going well, you can review your vision to give you the little push you need to come up with new ideas and keep going. Your vision can re-energize you. When difficult issues with employees, vendors, and customers arise, by considering your vision—really picturing it in your mind and imagining it occurring in your reality—it will rejuvenate you and remind you of your belief in your business.

The work of developing a vision gets you to exercise your mind. To take the time to think through the future of the business, what it should entail, and how much money it should make, requires you to work through thinking about the future in a big way. Just as exercising the body creates health and stamina, exercising the mind by working through the vision creates a stronger mind for you, the entrepreneur. A vision can keep people in a company working together harmoniously. When a business' vision is communicated to employees, it keeps them all on the same page. If your business has two or more owners, a vision can keep all of you from having arguments about the direction of the company.

A vision for your company keeps you at the forefront of decision-making. Rather than having the *necessity of making decisions* chasing after you like a dog biting at your heels, the vision helps to keep you in front of all the decisions that fall on your plate. Rather than the dog biting at your heels, you are more likely to take charge and be the person who rounds up stray dogs, putting them on a leash, and taking control.

So what's the big deal if you don't have a vision for your business? Haven't a lot of businesses become successful without having a vision? Not really. Probably 99.9 percent of people who start a business that becomes successful have a vision (either written on paper or in their minds) that fulfills this "vision requirement." So, what can happen if you don't create a vision?

- Without a vision, you can become just another employee of the company. You risk letting your thoughts and actions slip into *follower-mode*. Rather than being the leader you need to be, you can easily stop thinking and acting like a leader without that vision to guide every decision.
- Since the vision creates a reference point for you, without it you don't have the orientation needed to get back to the basics when you feel overwhelmed. If you had that reference point, it would provide a picture in your mind that you could go back to time after time to get re-oriented.
- When fear of change and fear of expansion set in, if you do not have a vision for your business, you will not have that picture in your thoughts to remind you of the goals and to get your thoughts and actions back on track.
- A lack of vision means that you have not exercised your mind. Just as a body gets flabby when not exercised, your mind can lose its ability to remain

sharp and focused when it has not been exercised to develop a vision.

Keep in mind that with all of the responsibilities that come with business ownership you can get mired in the details. You may barely have enough time to finish one immediate task and then another issue shows up on your plate. There is very little time to consider the long-term effects of a decision before a new decision-making opportunity arrives. If you want to succeed, you need to think about the future. Having the vision helps to create a balance between the future and the details of today. For your business to survive and thrive over time, you—the prime mover and shaker—must develop perspective.

When prescribing a drug, your doctor wants to know what other prescriptions you're taking because the wrong mix of drugs can be dangerous. He wants to see the whole picture and how the drugs interact so that chaos does not occur in your body. Likewise, for your business, you make one decision after another. You need time to get perspective (which includes going back to your vision) in order to ensure that you are not getting mired in chaos, which would lead to making poor calls for the business. By going back to your vision and gaining perspective, it helps you make good decisions at all times.

When you're making a six-course dinner for a party, it's exhausting work. There is the planning, shopping, cleaning, chopping, setting the atmosphere, the cooking, and making certain it is timed perfectly. While you're doing all of the work, you need to keep the vision in mind of how beautiful and delicious the dinner party will be and how your guests will enjoy it.

Likewise, in business, the vision comes from the driving force within you, the owner. During the period when you're striving to survive, you need a strong inner drive to keep you going to overcome the considerable obstacles that come along with business ownership. Those entrepreneurs who never lose sight of the original vision are those whose energy for the business never flags. This is because their eyes are always on the prize.

Turn Your Vision into Action

A vision for a business is as good as the paper it's written on—until the "author" does something with it. It needs to be implemented and, perhaps, tweaked over time.

The owner of a custom handbag company envisioned her business becoming known by women who enjoy accessories and textiles, first in the Midwest and later in the entire U.S. She described the vision for her business as involving sales growth, changes in the operations, and delegation of duties over time (so that she could eventually cut back on her long hours). She also included sponsoring a charity in her vision. Over time, she noted that her customers have been women who are individualistic and want to create their own sense of style. Early on, her business took on three additional managerial people over a three-year period, allowing her to cut back her hours to spend more time with her family. The first manager hired was responsible for the overall production and operations, the second hired was in charge of the design development, and the third hired took over the sales and customer service teams. In her first year in business, she chose a charity to work with regularly, and often promoted sales that directly impacted company donations to the charity. Originally, she envisioned growing the sales of the company by 30 percent in the second year, 20 percent in the following four years, and leveling off at a 10 percent to 12 percent growth rate in the ensuing years (and she planned to review the growth rate projections every year). She also worked into her schedule leadership development plans, including seminars, working with a business coach for three to six months every couple years, and reading select books and articles about leadership. After 10 years in business, she found she was on track. Her biggest challenges included continually motivating her key people and staying connected to the newest trends in the design and fashion world.

The owner of a computer parts distribution company envisioned being one of the top five distributors of his kind in the U.S after being in business for 15 years. In order to grow as fast as possible, and still keep things manageable, he decided to use outside manufacturer's representatives to sell his products. That way, he could find experienced sales reps with existing customer bases in all areas of the country. His vision included adding seven outside reps in the first year, seven in the second and third years, and three in the fourth year, to total 25 reps. He envisioned growing sales by 25 percent per year for the first seven years, and then leveling off to 7 percent to 10 percent growth in the following 10 years. To accommodate the ensuing growth that additional sales reps would bring with increased sales, he set his sights on increasing production with a larger warehouse staff and customer service staff, and securing offices and a warehouse that were a little larger than originally necessary. Later, he would add two to three distribution centers in other parts of the country. He saw himself as the chief creative officer who stayed at the forefront of new technology, while hiring people to oversee the day-to-day functions of the business. Personally, he saw himself owning a second home in Florida by his eighth year in business, with a staff that could "hold down the fort" for a week or two so that he could actually get away on a vacation from time to time. Over the first few years, he was not able to add as many manufacturer's reps in each year as he envisioned because it took more time than he expected to interview people from a distance in order to choose the right sales reps. Therefore, his sales growth rate was closer to 15 percent, which was slower than expected. It meant hiring the other team members at a slower rate, and he was able to purchase the Florida home a few years later than originally planned. So he tweaked his original vision to accommodate these changes in timing. For the most part, he was on track.

At the age of 35, a dentist had a vision for his practice to include three other dentists as employees, and expanding the number of patients by purchasing the accounts of a retiring dentist in his building by the time he had his own practice for 10 years. He saw himself retiring by age 60, selling his practice to another younger dentist. What he didn't count on was that, after buying out the practice of the retiring dentist in his building, several of the patients took the opportunity to find another dentist closer to their homes, as their loyalty and comfort was with their original dentist. Since he had already expanded the square footage of his practice, he had to work longer hours and perform the dental work himself before he could hire the three additional dentists he planned to hire and pay. He also had to spend more time figuring out how to add patients to his practice to fill up the appointment book so that he could hire the additional dentists to take on the added time slots. As he approached age 60, selling his practice would not yield the kind of money he wanted, so he continued working until he was 68. At that time he was finally able to sell his practice to another dentist. His original vision was a bit "off" in that he counted on keeping all of the patients from the practice he purchased. Had he been more realistic in that vision, he could have expanded his clinic to a smaller, more manageable size, thereby decreasing his expenses and perhaps reaching his goal of retiring by age 60.

In each of these cases, having a vision (a *realistic* vision) helped the entrepreneur's business take off. With a good vision, the owner was more likely to remain focused, keep his or her mind expanded while leading the business, and not get stuck in a "follower-mode."

Your Vision for Your Work and Your Life

When defining your vision for your work and your life, start with a "big picture" vision. Rather than getting involved in the details, think first in generalities. Once you have defined the high-level vision, you can work on defining the details. Here are some questions to ponder to get you started:
- What do you enjoy doing?
- In what areas would you say you are great?
- What are your strengths?

- What's possible?
- What do you believe you are here to accomplish?
- What is your business here to accomplish?

Next, take another step away from the previous questions and answer this: Even if you already love what you currently do in and for your business, if you could do whatever you wanted to do (and money was no object), what would you be doing over the course of a year? (Answer this for both your professional life and personal life.)

Now, bring your vision a little closer to home with some details.

- What do you want your business to achieve in the next three years?
- Consider areas such as sales, customers, changes in products/services, expansion, employees, strategic relationships, net profit, etc.
- What do you personally want to achieve in the next three years?
- Consider where you live, how you spend your time, marriage, other relationships, your stress level, your free time, academic pursuits, your emotional life, your spiritual life, etc.

Think Bigger

What is "thinking bigger"? It is stretching and exercising your mind, just as you stretch and exercise your body at a gym. It is turning small ideas into larger ideas. Sometimes, for a business, turning small ideas into larger ideas involves some type of expansion. That is the traditional thought, anyway. But for an entrepreneur who wants to increase profit and decrease stress, that is not the only definition. It can also mean expanding a simple idea into something that is more creative in order to achieve your goals.

How can you take what you know, what you do, and what you're great at, and turn it into something bigger and brighter? It must be "bigger and brighter" for you and your vision (not by anyone else's definition).

For example, Kevin owns a consulting business that did quite well for several years. He wanted to take the business to another level; however, he didn't want added stress. He was only willing to add more to his schedule on a very short-term basis. He needed to think and plan in a bigger way to get his business and his life where he wanted it to be. He knew there would be an initial investment of time and energy to get where he wanted to go, and he was willing to pay the temporary price.

After considering several options, he decided to focus on building strategic partnerships with other companies that serve the same customers. With that connection he planned to increase sales. He also wanted to use these relationships to find additional talent to hire for the work that would come from the added sales. Kevin was handling all of the employee and operations management, but with his planned growth, he intended to hire someone as the operations manager. Once all of this was in place, he planned to spend a little more time away from the business getting the R&R he needed.

Sandy had a micro business creating handmade invitations and announcements. People loved the work she did. The work was local and she had all the work she could handle. When challenged to "think bigger," Sandy accepted the challenge and considered teaching others how to do what she did. Since teaching classes would take more of her time, she also considered writing a book or manual that showed people how to make the items. With a book, she could reach many more people. The time she would need to devote to a book would be given just to write it; then it would multiply itself in sales. After considering writing the book, she also realized that producing DVDs would be another salable teaching tool to teach others how to do her work.

So, "thinking bigger" involves a new way of thinking in order to achieve your goals. Keep this in mind as you continue reading and working through the exercises in the Application sections. As you read the other chapters, new and bigger thoughts will come to you. Jot them down in your journal. As you reread your notes, your thoughts and ideas will gel and come to life. You have ideas in your subconscious that need a little prodding. Soon these individual ideas will be like marionettes that go from limp-to-life as you play the role of the puppeteer, orchestrating them to work together in a blended choreography.

Leadership Development & Growth

If you are going to be a leader for your business, you need to continually grow as a leader. As you develop your vision for your business, you need to include a picture of who you want to be as the leader of your business. This picture of yourself can change over time, just as your business will change over time. Make certain that your vision for yourself regarding leadership development is large enough to accommodate your business vision.

A friend of mine was in the middle of building a small koi pond in her backyard a few years ago. One day I was at her home before the pond was completed. It was partially installed and filled with water, but she didn't have the fish or plants yet. I looked outside and saw her big German shepherd frolicking and splashing in the pond. Boy, was she having a good time! She looked kind of goofy, though, that big dog cavorting in a little fish pond.

Some of us exist in a "place" that is too small for us to grow. Are you in too small of a place in order for you to:
- grow as a leader?
- achieve your goals?
- get out of a comfort zone?

For years I thought that goldfish stayed small and tiny. That's the size they were in our fish bowls. Then one day I found out that goldfish will only grow as large as their environment allows. In a larger pond, they will grow to their potential.

What "ponds" are keeping you from the growth you need to attain?

Or are you in a big pond but still feel like a little fish? Why be a little fish in a big pond?

What needs to be included in your vision regarding your own growth as a leader?

A Vision in History Applied to Today

In 1930, two brothers named Maurice and Dick moved from the East Coast to California in search of better opportunities. After holding a couple of jobs they opened a movie theater in a Los Angeles suburb. After running the theater for four years and not being able to turn a profit, they decided to switch gears, leave the theater business, and open a drive-in restaurant. Many people in the local area had cars and drive-in restaurants were a new idea.

After doing quite well with their new restaurant, they chose to move the business in 1940 to a different suburb that had a lot of growth. Their new location was a goldmine and the brothers were able to split an annual net profit of $50,000 a year. They made further changes to their restaurant in 1948, making it more casual, using paper products rather than ceramic and glass, and changed it from being a drive-in to a walk-in restaurant. They also created systems that helped their employees serve customers faster. By the mid-1950's, Maurice and Dick were splitting an annual net profit of $100,000 a year.

Next, they got the idea to market their restaurant concept through franchising. They sold fifteen franchises, and 10 of those new franchise owners opened restaurants. Actually, the brothers had a difficult time getting their franchise idea off the ground.

Who were these guys? Maurice and Dick were the original McDonald brothers. Sometimes when I have read their story, authors focus on how they "failed", and then Ray Kroc came in, bought them out, and made a success out of McDonald's Corporation.

But did the McDonald brothers really fail? It sounds to me like they had a pretty good life. They had a successful business, made a lot of money, and knew when to take new direction. So what if they couldn't do what Ray Kroc was able to do?

If the brothers had hung on to their business longer and tried to develop the franchise idea further, pouring more and more money into it, would they have increased their profit? Maybe. Would they have decreased their stress? No way. That amount of "Ray Kroc-like" growth was not where their expertise could take them.

Instead, they grew their business to a certain point and then sold it.

Did they increase their profit? Yes, they increased their profit by a lot! Not only did they make a good profit that gave them a great living from about the late 1930s and beyond, in 1961 Ray Kroc paid them $2.7 million for all rights to the McDonald's concept.

Did they decrease their stress? Yes!

The McDonalds brothers knew where to take their business and they knew when to change gears and sell it. I completely disagree with those authors who have said that these men failed.

I'm *not* saying you should go sell your business tomorrow. First, work through the principles in this book. Apply what you learn. Make changes to your business. Learn where *you* bring it together to increase your profit and decrease your stress.

Whether you choose to emulate Ray Kroc, the McDonald brothers, or some other entrepreneur is up to you. Please make sure your choice is worth the effort, sacrifice, and prize. If it makes you sick or dead, it's not worth it! Let's make certain that you enjoy both the ride *and* the prize.

You need to make sure that *your* vision leads you to increased profit *and* decreased stress, catapulting your business to new heights!

Sum it Up

If you've had some thoughts so far, jot them down in your journal. Use the Application section to go through the plans outlined there, step-by-step, and apply it to your business.

∗∗∗∗∗∗∗∗∗∗∗∗∗∗∗∗∗∗∗∗∗∗∗∗∗

After developing your vision, your next step is to focus on a few strategic areas of your business regarding how *you* conduct business.

Most entrepreneurs have areas of their business they find easy to run and other areas that are more difficult to handle. The next chapter covers many areas that business owners face and how to run them better, whether that involves time, stuff, bad habits, or a host of other issues.

Application

Your vision for your business (and for you as its owner) gets you thinking in terms of expansion, growth, and the future. A vision is all about the future. It involves picturing in your mind's eye various details about the business, its size, and the money it makes. When you get your thoughts set on a vision for your business, and then go back to review your vision time after time, you get your mind exercised in terms of forthcoming expansion and profit.

As you read in the chapter, "The work of developing a vision gets you to exercise your mind." To take the time to think through the future of the business, what it should entail, and how much money it should make, requires you to work through thinking about the future in a big way. Just as exercising the body creates health and stamina, exercising the mind by working through the vision creates a stronger mind for you, the entrepreneur.

Your Vision for Your Work and Your Life

When defining your vision for your work and your life, start with a "big picture" vision. Rather than getting involved in the details, think first in generalities. Once you have defined the high-level vision, you can work on defining the details. Here are some questions to ponder to get you started:

    2.1   What do you enjoy doing?

2.2 In what areas would you say you are great?

2.3 What are your strengths?

2.4 What's possible?

2.5 What do you believe you are here to accomplish?

2.6 What is your business here to accomplish?

2.7 If you could do whatever you wanted to do (and money was no object), what would you be doing over the course of a year? (Answer this for both your professional life and personal life.)

Now, bring your vision a little closer to home with some details.

2.8 What do you want your business to achieve in the next three years? (Consider areas such as sales, customers, changes in products/services, expansion, employees, strategic relationships, net profit, etc.)

2.9 What do you personally want to achieve in the next three years? (Consider where you live, how you spend your time, marriage, other relationships, your stress level, your free time, academic pursuits, your emotional life, your spiritual life, etc.)

Think Bigger

Read through the "Think Bigger" part of the chapter again if it's been a while since you read it.

2.10 What products or services does your business provide to customers today?

2.11 How might what you offer be combined with other products or services that would add profit to the business?

2.12 Brainstorm some ways that you might "think bigger" for your business:

2.13 Are there any other businesses that you could partner with in order to sell more?

Leadership Development & Growth

2.14 Before you owned your business, describe how you were encouraged to develop (or discouraged from developing) your leadership skills in previous careers and jobs:

2.15 How would you describe your leadership of your business so far?

More to Consider

2.16 Like the McDonald brothers, where do you believe is the dividing line between making a great profit but having an overstressed life vs. having the entrepreneurial life that gives you plenty of free time but doesn't bring in enough money?

2.17 Write your thoughts about the following:

A. What are you currently doing that you enjoy?

B. What did you identify that you enjoy doing that is not currently part of your life?

C. How can you make a change so that you are doing that?

   D. How are you currently using your greatness?

   E. How would you like to use your greatness?

   F. How are you utilizing your strengths?

   G. How would you like to use your strengths?

   H. As you consider what is possible, how might you put it into practice?

   I. Are you currently doing what you believe you are here to accomplish?

J. If not, what can you do to change that?

K. Is your business currently doing what you believe it exists to accomplish?

L. If not, what can you do to change that?

M. Is there anyone (either currently or in your past) who discouraged you from being successful? Write in your journal how they discouraged you and how that affected your beliefs about success.

2.18 Is there anyone who encouraged you to be successful, and to do so while reaching your own goals and dreams? In what ways did they do that?

2.19 What has gotten in your way of increasing your profit?

2.20 What has gotten in your way of decreasing your stress?

2.21 What might you do to keep all of that from getting in your way in the future?

2.22 If you achieve catapulting your business to new heights of profit (while also decreasing your stress level), what will that mean for your business and your life?

Change Your Way of Doing Business

*"An entrepreneur tends to bite off
a little more than he can chew, hoping
he'll quickly learn how to chew it.*

—Roy Ash

*M*uch like how astronauts see the earth from a spaceship, as a whole picture with little-to-no detail, a vision provides a wide framework for the business without detail. This is why you worked on the business vision first, in order to create a big picture into which details can be entered later.

Whereas the last chapter was about developing a personal vision for your business, this chapter gets into the nuts and bolts of how you can take yourself and your business through a strategy to improve yourself as an entrepreneur and your business as a winning operation. The vision gives you the big picture for the business. Over time, it continues to provide perspective, anchoring why you are in business and what your business exists to accomplish in the world. The details, and the plans you put in place to work out those details, bring your vision to life.

Creating entrepreneurial plans is more like sitting in a car and needing to get somewhere that you've never been before, but having a detailed roadmap to guide you. When taking a trip to a new place and reading a roadmap, you decipher where to go and how to best get there. A roadmap provides many details, including various choices of direction in order to reach the same goal. Many times when reading a map you'll notice, for example, three different ways to get to the same place. But because you haven't traveled those roads before, you don't quite know which of the three is best for your journey.

Visions are more inspirational than plans and details because, with a vision, you see the beauty of something (like the astronaut's view of the entire earth). The beauty of something can pull you along when the going gets tough. It is more inspirational than anything else connected to the business.

A roadmap, on the other hand, as you study it, gives you details, not beauty. It is not inspirational. It is vital, though, when you're at a crossroads and have a decision to make. (While a vision will help to give you general direction, it will not help you make detailed decisions at a crossroads.) The accurate details of terrain that you find on a roadmap helps you with the details and decisions that are immediately in front of you.

Putting together a strategy for a business is as important as having a roadmap for a trip because *business* is all about making decisions *for* the business (and for you, yourself) all the time. You would not want to do business without a plan any more than you would take a cross country trip into unknown territory without a map.

So this chapter takes you through a number of journeys intended to strengthen your ability to be a great strategist for your company.

Creating a plan and working at it is crucial to your success. It is a lot like an explorer drawing a map in order to successfully complete a journey. In order to catapult your business to new heights, you need to make room for both creating a plan *and* working it into your life. Exchanging certain old activities, habits, and priorities for new ones will help you achieve your goals. Before you can create a new way of thinking and planning, you need to figure out what gets in your way and what to do about it.

Once you determine what gets in your way and start to change it, you can strategize new ways of thinking, planning, and executing that make room in your life for more success with less stress. A plan will give you more mental and physical energy to meet your goals.

Achieving some of the goals covered in this chapter will require you to attain the goals outlined in other chapters, such as *Delegate to Generate More Success*. Keep this in mind as you develop the leadership skills outlined in this chapter.

Make Room for More Profit in Your Life

What is getting in your way that is adding stress to your life and keeping you from more profit? Even if you can easily identify those activities, people, or "stuff", it may feel difficult (or even impossible) to imagine how to remove those stressors permanently. If you are going to reach new levels of success, you need to *make room* for more profit in your life by making changes that decrease stress. Let's look at some major areas that trip up most businesspeople and how to overcome them.

Tackle Tasks & Activities

The "tyranny of the urgent" gets the best of most of us. Urgent tasks constantly crowd out the most important activities you need to accomplish for your business. That is, until you take control of the urgent tasks and become the master of your time.

Traditional thinking says that only employees waste their time and that business owners never do. In truth, however, the boss also fritters away time. Many distractions that crop up daily seem important when they occur. You can always make an argument for how important some activity is to you. Let's briefly look at a few typical activities that can easily waste your time.

One of the time wasters that can crop into a business owner's day is being on the Internet. Between keeping current in your field, reading the news, checking the competition, doing research, and reading and responding to e-mail, you can easily spend much more time on the web than you intend. I've often found myself expecting to spend 20 minutes doing Internet tasks, but that quickly became two hours. I started keeping a timer at my desk, nicknamed the "Internet Timer," to keep me from spending too much time online. I literally set the Internet Timer for the amount of time I want to be online, and when the bell rings, I switch to doing something else.

Another time waster is unnecessary socializing in the office. While a certain amount of socializing is helpful to business relationships, too much just takes up valuable time. I've known people who own construction and remodeling businesses who spent too much time talking (in the social sense) with vendors and customers, doctors who spent a lot of time chatting (beyond polite conversation), and I've seen restaurateurs on the television show "Kitchen Nightmares" who spent way too much time conversing with customers in the dining room. When you were an employee, do you recall your co-workers spending too much time socializing? What do you think could have fixed that problem? What if regular lunches outside of the office were scheduled, say, once or twice a month? That way people would get a longer time to talk without taking up too much work time to socialize. If you have a personal issue with using too much of your time for social talking (with vendors, customers, employees, or the mailman), consider how you will change that and get that time back. And hold your thoughts about this until later in this chapter for the section that concentrates on your habits.

Too much focus on getting through mounds of paper is another time waster that business owners are faced with. You need to get assistance with it before it steals too much time from your day.

Some people with certain types of businesses spend too much time running errands for the business. Especially businesses where the owner is out calling on customers or overseeing jobs at customer sites, it is very easy (once their car is on the road) to make several stops for the business that cut into time that could be used more strategically.

If you don't learn to take charge of your time, little nuisances throughout the day will take up huge chunks of time that you can never get back again. Even though tomorrow is another day with a whole new set of minutes and hours in which to try again, your competitor (who has already mastered his time) focused on the important activities yesterday and then got the big deal signed today. You lose.

Business owners can easily get swamped in tasks and activities that pull them away from making money for the business. Has this ever happened to you? Sometimes, certain tasks seem *easy* to do or they are your strength, so you use your precious time to complete them (even though the easy tasks don't contribute much to the bottom line profit, either directly or indirectly). For example, the owner of an auto repair shop may spend too much time working on cars himself when he could train four men to work on the cars instead and invest his time in increasing sales and lowering expenses for his auto shop.

Other times, it seems as if there is no one available to assist in the myriad tasks that must be handled at all businesses. Owners who have not invested some time in learning to delegate tasks wisely end up with too many tasks on their plates. Entrepreneurs who spend their time unwisely may lose business or miss opportunities that could improve their businesses and make more money.

On the other hand, when you take charge of your time, you learn to focus on the tasks and activities that bring you the most money for the hours and minutes you invest.

If you're going to run a successful business, you need to really get the idea that *time equals money* burned into your brain. Your employees (except, perhaps, salespeople) get paid whether the business has profit or not. You, however, get paid from the profit. Consequently, no matter how tempting it is to go off on a tangent with extra activities that do not bring the business a great return for your time, it is incumbent on you to identify the activities that give you the best return for your time.

There are some pitfalls of not weeding through your business activities and choosing them more wisely. For example, you can wind up with a schedule full of tasks that continually pull you away from activities that could bring you a lot more profit. You may have a preoccupation with insignificant matters with no time left for long-term planning. If you try to do both your high return activities and low return activities, you'll realize belatedly that "time" has to come from somewhere. For many entrepreneurs, that usually means sleep time will be robbed in order to do it all. Ultimately, sleep deprivation can cause you to make more and more poor choices. By not identifying the activities that bring you the highest return for your time, you won't be able to focus on those activities and delegate the rest. You'll be too inundated with a long *to-do* list that will crowd out the activities that would bring you the most profit.

When a business owner analyzes her activities in order to eventually focus on those that give her the highest return for her time, and then makes adjustments to her schedule to include more and more of those high yield activities (*"high yield"* meaning the activities give her the highest profit for her time), she'll see that the business is making more money. Perhaps she'll spend more time on communications that result in new customers and better relationships with existing customers (which leads to more sales). She might make certain that employees are well-trained (maybe she hires someone to train them and to create a really good employee manual) and that vendors understand what they need to accomplish. And she might find she's spending more time on strategic planning than she ever did before and less time on smaller matters that an employee or vendor can handle. All of these activities easily result in higher profit, mostly because the entrepreneur figured out how to take charge of her time.

To begin taking charge of *your* time, you will identify your current tasks and activities. Throughout the next week, take some time to write out all of the tasks that take you more than 10 minutes to complete. Write out as many as possible. This is a brainstorming activity where you will just list out your activities without judgment. Some of the tasks that take more than 10 minutes of your time might include the following examples:

- Taking phone calls
- Returning voicemail messages
- Reading e-mail
- Responding to e-mail
- Reading mail
- Responding to mail
- Reading memos
- Responding to memos
- Reading faxes
- Responding to faxes
- Creating proposals for prospects
- Meeting with prospects
- Following-up with prospects
- Closing sales
- Building customer relationships
- Handling customer inquiries
- Training employees

- Handling employee issues
- Maintaining employee benefit plans
- Research and development
- Handling operations issues
- Planning and innovation
- Strategic planning for the short-term
- Strategic planning for the long-term
- Forecasting budgets
- Reviewing financial statements
- Reviewing outstanding receivables

Add your own activities. Then for each activity, write about how much time you spend on it weekly.

Here is an example:

Task or Activity	Amount of Time Weekly
Creating proposals for prospects	15 hours
Reading & responding to e-mail	5 hours
Building customer relationships	4 hours

Once you complete your list, it's time to analyze it. Which activities on your list are the most important for you? In other words, which give you a higher yield and better returns (*more profit potential*) than any other activities?

- Highlight three to five that give you the best returns.

- Approximately how much time do you spend weekly on each of the highlighted activities?

- Total the amount of time spent on all of the highlighted activities.

- On average, how much time do you spend on your business each week?

- Next, calculate the percentage of the total time spent on your important, highlighted tasks to the total amount of time spent on your business. What is the percentage?

- What would happen if the percent of time spent on those high yield activities increased to between 50 percent and 80 percent of the total?

You might find that certain *subsets* of activities give you a high yield return. For example, if you respond to certain phone calls, e-mails, and other communications from *particular strategic customers*, the time spent on those responses for those customers brings you a lot of money. The problem may be sifting through all of the voicemails, e-mails, regular mail, and faxes from *everyone* in order to find those *particular customers*. In a case like this example, could someone else do the sifting? In other words, could an employee be trained to go through the communications, find those that are significant and strategic, and forward those communications to you for your response? That way, your time spent on the activities of "reviewing and responding to communications" is focused only on those subsets that give your business the highest yield for your time investment.

Your high yield activities have the most impact on your business, on your revenue, and/or on your profit. (I say "and/or" because some of your activities may *reduce your expenses* significantly, which gives you more profit, but they don't affect your sales/revenue). Most likely, the high yield activities also energize you and remind you why you are in business. Set a goal to increase the total percent of your time spent on your most important high yield activities to equal 50 percent of your time in about four months from now. Then try to increase that percentage to 80 percent of your time 12 months from now.

Are You a "Yes-Man" (or Woman)?

Think back to a movie or television show you've seen when a character constantly says "yes" to any request made of him. Most of the time, and perhaps most humorously, the requester is the person's boss (and he feels that he just cannot say "no" every time the boss makes a request). But the person making the request could be any number of people. It could be co-workers or employees who still don't understand how to do their jobs well (or who don't *want* to do their jobs, such as certain characters in *Dilbert* cartoons). It could be customers who constantly call, wanting assistance (without paying extra for it). It could be someone in the community who wants the movie character's time. The point is, the character in the movie or television show says "yes" to just about everyone who asks for their time, even if it steals time away from their most profitable activities.

Perhaps you know someone in "real life" who has a hard time saying "no." Maybe the word sounds too harsh or too final. Or maybe someone in their past said "no" to them too many times and they told themselves that they would never do that to another person.

Is it difficult for *you* to say "no" to people when they request your time? (If you're not sure, ask your spouse or a close friend what they think.) If so, think about the people who ask for your time most often.

- What do they ask you to fit into your schedule?
- How do these activities measure up to your high yield activities?
- What is the worst thing that could happen with each person if you started to say "no" to half of their requests?
- Would there be a way for you to "transfer" their requests to an employee to handle?

If saying the word "no" sounds too harsh, try saying other words and phrases such as "Not now, maybe in a few days," or "I'll have to get back to you on that later." And as you work through this entire chapter, consider how important it is to the life of your business (and to your physical and mental health) for you to focus your time on your high-profit activities and to leave the rest to others. That should motivate you to find new ways to stop saying "yes" to every request that comes your way.

Tame the Information Tiger

When you come to your workplace every workday, the one thing you bring with you is your "quality of mind." Whatever "state" it's in, that's what you bring to the table. It is an accumulation of the previous day's "stuff" (and perhaps the day before that and the day before that). Do you find that the "quality of mind" you bring to your business daily is high or low?

The more time goes on, the more we are bombarded by information. Just a couple generations ago, the bulk of information coming into peoples' lives was from the newspaper (if they chose to read it) and radio. When they opened their personal mail, they found a few letters and bills (or maybe just one postcard from a friend on vacation). Their business mail did not include much more than that, either. Their telephones did not have call waiting, voicemail, or answering machines. The next generation added television and a little more information in their postal mail. Television in metropolitan areas included three major network stations, perhaps two or three local stations, and PBS.

We, however, are on information overload. Our regular mailbox alone is filled with too much information. Our telephones have call waiting, voicemail, or an answering machine (and remote access to messages), making it difficult to miss a call. E-mail and the Internet added a whole new venue to "too much information." Certainly some people know exactly how many television stations they can get on their cable or satellite access, but it boggles my mind. Cell phones allow us to be accessible almost any time in any place. If we are not near our computer to receive our e-mail, news, or stock quotes, we can receive it on our cell phone.

I like having the convenience of nearly all of these methods of communication. If I need to get exact data to someone (or to a group of people), e-mail is fabulous. It's quick, it's cheap, and it's clearer than a telephone message. I'm glad that I don't have to miss a telephone call, thanks to voicemail or my answering machine, and even call waiting. My cell phone is handy when I'm away from my office or home, and I feel it is a type of "insurance" in case my car stalls.

Some brave souls I know choose to not have access to some of these tools. I know people who have voicemail for their business, but they do not have an answering machine, voicemail, or call waiting at home. Some people have told me they do not tune in to the news at all (or not very often). Several people I know do not use e-mail, or, if they have it for business, someone else goes through it and prints the important e-mails for them to read. A couple people have told me they do not have a television.

While I do not believe the answer to reducing "information overload" is this extreme for everyone, I do believe some tweaking is in order to lessen the stressor called "TMI" ("too much information"). TMI will reduce your "quality of mind" very quickly. It will fill your brain with too much unnecessary data. When your quality of mind is low, your productivity suffers. Therefore, your business is affected negatively by TMI.

So what can you do about TMI? First, take a few minutes to identify the factors of "too much information" that cause *you* stress or that cause you, your thoughts, or your energy to be pulled away from more important goals. What information sources get in your way?

Here are some examples:
- News (in any format)
- Television
- Radio
- E-mails
- Regular mail
- Cell phones
- Text messages
- Internet

Second, determine *how* those sources get in your way. You do not need to spend a lot of time on this. However, spend about three to five minutes on each information source thinking through *how* that information adds stress to your life and/or *from which* important activities it takes time. Too much of this stuff takes up time and takes up "data space" in your head. The more information that comes at you, the less time and space you'll have for important matters of your business that need attention. If the information coming at you is not managed, it will squeeze out crucial items that you really need to focus on, such as how to make the next big sale or how to make adjustments to the business in the short-term and long-term to increase the bottom line.

Next, figure out how you are going to cut down on the particular information coming into your life from that source. Set a goal for yourself and be realistic. This is not too different from changing your diet or changing other habits. Ask yourself, "Is it better for me to cut that stressor out slowly, or should I go 'cold turkey'?"

Some of these may need different types of adjustments. If your stressor is e-mail, perhaps you need to have an assistant go through your e-mail for you, print out the important messages, and give them to you. If that is not possible, another method may work for you. E-mail was a stressor for me because I felt I had to open everything. Most of the time I could not figure out the importance of the e-mail just from the subject line and opening it was the only way to find out. While I did not read the entire text from start to finish, I read enough of each e-mail to take up a lot of time. Finally I had enough. Now I do not even open many of the e-mails in my inbox. If I know that I do not want to read it, I delete it immediately. If I am not certain if I want to read it or not, I leave it unopened.

For your business and personal life, there may be other sources of information (such as e-mail) that are still necessary. Your goal is to keep it from:

- becoming "too much information"
- being a stressor
- taking time away from more important activities

When you tame the information tiger, all of those "information stressors" take a back seat and obey you. With all of that data tamed, you have more time to focus on the critical issues affecting your business and your profit.

Conquer Clutter

Is your office or workspace filled with clutter? Does clutter make it difficult to get work done well? Clutter is any type of papers and other office supplies, plus specific items related to your business, that take up room in your workspace. This includes stacks of paper, binders, files, and reports. For a specific business, such as an auto mechanic's business, it includes auto parts and other inventory that take up the space and countertops where everyone works.

When there is clutter, it can be more difficult for you to make clear decisions and prioritize for the business. Clutter has both a physical effect and a psychological effect: It takes up space on your desk and space in your mind. When it takes up space in your mind, it steals room from your thoughts that could better serve you by making room for thoughts about your business that make you more money.

By clearing out physical clutter, you also clear out a creative space in your mind that can be better used to lead your business with clarity. In addition, if you keep your place virtually clutter-free, it will also help your employees by creating a place for them where they can think more clearly.

If you look around your workspace and see clutter, it may be keeping you from your ultimate productivity level. Just like dealing with "too much information," it's time to do something about it. *Conquer clutter* by starting your decluttering process in one room or office space at a time.

Paper clutter

For paper items, get an "inbox" and put it on a desk. When you don't have time to put papers away or you're not certain where it should go, put it in your inbox. Occasionally, sort through it. (That could mean weekly, monthly, or whenever you get tired of looking at it.)

When you are ready to go through the papers, sort them into the following piles or groups:

- File
- Throw out
- Read first
- Not sure yet

Once you have sorted your papers into these groups, it's time to deal with them.

- File the "file pile" right away. You may find it best in your office to have someone else file papers. In that case, get another inbox, label it "File", and place all of your "to file" papers there for one of your employees to file.
- Next, throw out the "throw out" pile. Just put it in a garbage bag and get it out of your office.
- Put the "read" items in a basket or file folder, and put it on your desk or other space in your office. Carve out some "reading time" to get through it. Take some of it with you whenever you are going somewhere that you will have to wait (such as the doctor's or dentist's office, barbershop or salon, etc.). Keep a pen handy. When you finish reading it, write on it "file" or "toss." When you get back to your office, either put it in your "File" inbox, or throw it out right away.
- Set the "not sure" group aside and come back to it within 24 hours to decide what to do with each piece (file, throw out, or read).

Clutter Other Than Paper

For items other than paper, gather all of the items on one or two large tables. If it helps, use boxes to place these items into as you pick them up throughout the office. (The boxes that copy paper comes in are great for this purpose.)

Sort these items in a similar manner as you did for paper:

- Put away
- Throw out
- Not sure yet

The goal for items other than paper is to either *put it away* or *throw it out*. If you find that your group of "not sure yet" items is growing, stop sorting and go through that group. Make decisions about this stuff. Ask yourself some questions:

- What is it about this item that is keeping me from throwing it out right now?
- What might I/we need this for in the future?
- Can something else be used in its absence?
- If we keep this, where should we put it today?
- Do we need more cabinet or closet space? If so, how can we get it soon?

After you sort through the items:

- Throw out the "throw out" items *now*.
- Put away the "put away" items as soon as possible.

"I Don't Even Have Time to Sort Through All This Stuff!"

If that subtitle sounds like what you were just thinking, then perhaps it's time you hired a professional organizer to sort through your papers and other items. A professional organizer can also help you set up a system to *keep* your office clutter-free. Find a professional organizer who lives in your area. Check your telephone directory's yellow pages under "Organizing Services." Or check the National Association of Professional Organizers at www.napo.net, and check their "Find an Organizer" link to locate someone in your area. Do it! Now!

Habits: Out With the Bad, In With the Good

Bad habits are any routines that are counterproductive, keeping you from doing your best. At first, they creep into your schedule and don't seem to make much of a negative difference to your business. However, they build up over time and steal time away from your productivity and high yield tasks.

When you do something over and over, it becomes habitual. That is because the action is reinforced every time it's done. This principle applies to all habits, good and bad. First, let's look at bad habits, including some typical examples, and how they affect your business.

Bad habits and tendencies can get in the way of your success. In order to make room for more profit, you may need to clear out some habits from your life. When entrepreneurs don't tackle their bad habits, those actions take up time and thought space in the brain. Bad habits waste a lot of energy and brain power (your valuable "internal resources") that could be better used to lead your business. When you overcome bad habits, you will have more time and "brain space" available for leadership.

Do you tend to put things off until the last minute? Do you constantly look for extensions to your commitments because you are not going to make the deadline? Perhaps you have a habit of procrastination. If so, take a look at your current projects. Are there too many projects on your plate? What gets in the way of tackling your projects and activities sooner rather than later? Do you prefer to mull them over for a while? If so, is there a way you can let your thoughts simmer without putting the projects and commitments on the back burner for too long?

Do you try to do things perfectly every time? Does your need for perfection keep you from getting projects done on time? If so, perfectionism may be your habit. Attempt to view your projects through realistic glasses. Given the time and resources at your disposal, what is realistic? What is reasonable? What parts of the project must be perfect, and what parts must not? Give yourself deadlines and do not waver.

As the chief-owner, chief-manager, and chief-creator of your business, do you have difficulty letting other people do their jobs (and even make mistakes)? Do you ever re-do your employees' work? Would any of your employees say that you are a "micro-manager"? Being a micro-manager is very stressful in the long-run. How can you possibly wear the number of hats required in order to micro-manage your people? If you see yourself in this verbal reflection, take some time to consider what it costs you and your business to manage in this way.

Do you tend to be easily distracted by anything (or certain things) while you're working, such as others peoples' conversations, searching the web for something in particular, or particular interruptions? Try to identify these things and figure out some ways to keep yourself from being distracted. If you have identified any bad habits of your own, it is time to make some changes and develop good habits as a replacement.

Certainly, to get where you are now you have developed many good habits that have served you well. Good habits in business are behaviors that lead you to higher profit. Again, they're called "habits" because they've become regular routines that kick into automatic gear because you've practiced them over and over until you don't even need to think about them much in order to practice them. When we don't develop good habits, we leave the door open to nurture bad habits.

Some examples of good habits that affect your business include being on time, booking regular time for strategic planning, sticking to a schedule, letting other people manage their own responsibilities, an exercise routine, eating healthy food, and drinking water instead of soda or coffee.

Studies have shown it takes about four weeks to form a new habit. When you develop good habits, you set yourself up for success because the good habits crowd out any chance of bad habits getting a foothold. Your good habits establish a routine that uses your time effectively and allows you to use your thoughts to clearly manage your business.

Perhaps in the last few minutes you've thought of some of your bad habits. What habits do you have that you would like to change? How do you think you could change them? What would be the fastest way possible?

And maybe you've thought of some good habits you would like to start that would improve your leadership performance. What are those good habits? How can you start to make a change to develop each of them into automatic habits over the next month?

Catapult Your Business and Increase Your Profit

As you eliminate activities and habits that add stress to your life and get in the way of your success, you can add new ways of doing business to increase your profit. How you *work, focus,* and *think* has a lot to do with your success.

Prioritize and Focus

You are probably a "multi-tasker". Most business owners and executives I know must delve into several projects at once. Some people are better than others at handling a number of tasks at once. In your multi-tasking, have you ever worked on so many projects at a time that you were spread too thin and didn't do any of them very well?

Even for people who are good multi-taskers, they can get in an overload position and start to drop the balls. When people are depending on you to do a good job, whether it's customers, investors, line operators, or your business partner, handling too much at once can be costly.

Mike owns a manufacturing company in southern Indiana. He grew up in a large family where everyone was expected to help out and look out for one another. Because of this upbringing, Mike is a pretty good multi-tasker. He started at a young age to balance several activities at once without getting much help from his parents to do it. Since he was the second oldest of eight, he was one of the kids who was expected to help the younger ones while handling his own school work, chores, and social activities. Later, he applied this skill to his business. For years, Mike prided himself on being able to handle many activities at one time.

Multi-tasking in a family is different from multi-tasking in a manufacturing facility, however. Mike found out over several years that his multi-tasking skills have a limit. Once it's saturated, his effectiveness goes downhill. He learned that he must let go of some tasks along the way or else he will not do any of them well.

You are the person who determines *how much is too much* for you to handle at once. You need to set priorities and focus on them.

Of all the projects you have to balance, try working on no more than three to five at a time. This ensures that you will do them well and that you will not burn out. When you put one of those projects aside, you can pick up another.

Is it hard to choose just three to five projects to work on at a time? Go back to the activities you highlighted earlier in this chapter. Which projects fit into your high yield activities? What are the priorities? What really needs to be done first? Consider choosing projects that enhance your current customer relationships or that put you in contact with future customers. Work on three to five of those first. When you are finished, pick up another project to complete. This method ensures that you prioritize and focus on your high-yield activities and that you do not burn out in the process.

The "Three-Day" Plan

If you want to further increase your profit and decrease your stress, you will want to change the way you divvy up your days. When you divide your time into three different types of days, *Focus days, Buffer days*, and *Free days*, you will further learn how to focus your energy to make more money and to relax on other days to reduce your stress level.

Focus days

Focus days are for working *in* your business. Earlier you identified the top three to five important activities you perform for your business. These activities will tend to get crowded out by urgent matters. *On focus days, concentrate on performing only your high-yield activities.*

The idea is to maximize what you do best. Your business will benefit from your concentration. This is an area where you will focus on increasing profit.

On your focus days, you will not necessarily leave out activities such as returning calls. Return e-mails and phone calls if they fit into your top, high-yield activities. For example, if your high-yield activities include building relationships with current customers, return customer phone calls and e-mails in order to build those relationships.

Buffer days

Buffer days are for working *on* your business. Buffer days are for staff meetings, vendor meetings, following up on phone calls and e-mails, doing paperwork, and doing the activities that have prevented you from doing great work that makes an impact. Also, your focus days will generate other work that can be completed on your buffer days.

Free days

Free days are for yourself, family, socializing, recreation, intellectual pursuits, and spiritual activities. On these days, you do no business-related work, no e-mail, and no money management. Free days allow you to remove stress from your life.

How Do You Implement the "Three-Day" Plan?

If you take some time to implement the "Three-Day" Plan, you will ease yourself into it and make adjustments where necessary. You will also need to work with your team as you implement this plan. Help them understand the plan and why you are doing it.

Try to start with one Focus day per week. After a month, increase your Focus days to two days per week. Eventually, you will want your most important activities to take up 50 percent to 80 percent of your workdays, and the buffer activities to take up 20 percent to 50 percent of your workdays. (So that goal would work out to 2 1/2 to 4 days per week being Focus days for the high-yield tasks!)

If starting with a full Focus day seems like too much, start by spending either the morning or the afternoon just on your Focus activities. Later, build it up to 75 percent focus activities on Focus days, and eventually spend the entire Focus day on focus activities. Eventually, you will find a balance that works well for you and that generates more profit.

Change Your Thinking

How do you need to *think* for your business? How does your business *need* for you to think? We all have "thinking strengths" that we culled over the years and we will tend to gravitate to that strength when doing business. Most people's thinking styles fall into one of four categories: The *futuristic thinker,* the *big-picture thinker,* the *strategic thinker,* and the *current thinker.*

Which of the following "thinker" categories do you see as your tendency and your strength?

Futuristic Thinker

A futuristic thinker easily focuses on the next five to ten years. This is great because your business needs for you to consider the long term; if you get too caught up in the business' current events it can keep you from your vision and long-term growth. However, the futuristic thinker typically has a hard time with the "here-and-now." He gives very little thought to what is happening with the business and with people today.

Big-Picture Thinker

The big-picture thinker constantly sees the entire business and how it relates to other influences. Your business needs for you to keep the big picture in mind. If you get too bogged down in the details, your business will lose. The big-picture thinker sees the forest, but not necessarily the trees. Her thoughts can go from "problem" to "solution" in seconds. Unfortunately, because she has a difficult time with details, she fails to see the obstacles in her way that need to be addressed in order to arrive at the *best* solution.

Strategic Thinker

People who think strategically easily keep their finger on many areas at once. Your business needs for you to consider several areas of strategy for increasing sales, servicing your customers, developing leaders, eyeing costs, considering an exit strategy, etc. The strategic thinker constantly considers how he can create new deals and new ways of doing business, how he can develop leaders, keep an eye on costs, and even how and when he can sell the business some day and go do something else with the cash. An excess of this type of thinking can lead to current issues being ignored, which might lead to unhappy customers or unhappy employees.

Current Thinker

Current thinkers concentrate on what is happening today and next week. They can clearly identify problems and arrive at solutions. Your business needs for you to focus on what is happening now, what has recently occurred, and the next year or two. The business also needs for you to learn from its recent history and apply what you learned to "now." Sometimes, getting caught up in the next five to ten years while ignoring "today" can hurt the business. After getting the *current thinking* down pat, you can pass the business *current events* on to others and focus more on the future. Current thinkers can "put out fires" better than anyone else. However, too much of "current thinking" keeps the business too ingrained in the "now" rather than preparing the business for any part of the future. It can be too shortsighted.

What is Your Business Thinking Style?

In order to "change your thinking," it involves, first, identifying the category where you typically find yourself; second, purposely practicing getting your thoughts into each of the other four types of thinking; and third, applying the other types of thinking to your business.

Which of these styles describe you and your "thinking" strengths most accurately? If your strength is primarily in one of these areas, it is a good idea to "exercise your business muscle" in the other areas as well. Too much concentration in one area may occur at the expense of the others.

Focusing on any of these types too much can be detrimental to your business. For example, focusing too much on the future can keep you from seeing what is right in front of you and from seeing an issue that requires your attention now. Likewise, if you do not want to know about details (no matter how important), you can miss something crucial that will impact your sales or expenses in a significant way.

Changing your thinking also involves *thinking vertically* and *thinking horizontally*. To "think vertically" is to think deeply about an issue or situation, or to think at a new level. For people who tend to get bogged down in the details, "thinking vertically" means focusing on the "big picture" and "seeing the forest for the trees". For people who tend to only see the big picture, thinking vertically means getting involved in some details in order to gain a new understanding that helps you make better decisions.

To "think horizontally" is to think of additional possibilities at the same level. For example, if you are working on "the bigger picture" of an issue, horizontal thinking gets you to generate more ideas and solutions at that level.

If you don't change your thinking style (and stay stuck in the same style) you run the risk of not planning the future of your business very well, not seeing all of the business at one time (in order to make good decisions that affect several areas of the business), or not being able to make good decisions today and solve today's problems. When you take some time to evaluate your thinking style and change it, you give your business more opportunity to grow because you can see the business and all of its issues with a fresh perspective.

Strategically Plan Your Changes

A lot of the work of being an entrepreneur starts with you. How you spend your time, learning to say "no" to some people and tasks, getting a handle on all of the information coming your way, conquering clutter, changing bad habits into good habits, prioritizing your work, spending more and more time on high yield activities, and changing your thinking will go a long way toward lowering your stress, increasing your profit, and propelling your business to a whole new level.

Sum it Up

Make sure you take some time to think through what you've read in this chapter. Use a journal and the Application section to write out your thoughts, what you identify as areas that need to change, and the all-important commitments regarding how you will implement change.

****

Next, you will consider how your business is structured, how it *needs* to be structured, and how the systems that run the business can be changed in order to maximize profit.

Application

Below is a list of tasks and activities that many business owners find on their "to do" list that usually take longer than 10 minutes to complete. Add any more that are typically on your "to do" list at the end. Next to each, write in about how much time you spend on each task weekly.

Task or Activity	Amount of Time Weekly
Taking phone calls	
Returning voicemail messages	
Reading e-mail	
Responding to e-mail	
Reading mail	
Responding to mail	
Reading memos	
Responding to memos	
Reading faxes	
Responding to faxes	
Creating proposals for prospects	
Meeting with prospects	
Following-up with prospects	
Closing sales	
Building customer relationships	
Handling customer inquiries	
Training employees	
Handling employee issues	
Maintaining employee benefit plans	
Research and development	
Handling operations issues	
Planning and innovation	
Strategic planning for the short-term	
Strategic planning for the long-term	
Forecasting budgets	
Reviewing financial statements	
Reviewing outstanding receivables	

3.1 Go back to the list and highlight or circle 3 to 5 that give you a higher yield and better returns (*more profit potential*) than any other activities. List them below with the amount of time spent weekly on these high-yield tasks:

3.2 What is the total number of hours on all of those high-yield tasks?

3.3 On average, how much time do you spend in and on your business each week?

3.4 Divide the total amount of time you spend weekly on your high yield activities by the total amount of time you spend weekly on the business and write that percentage below:

3.5 What do you think would happen if the percent of time spent on those high-yield activities increased to 50 percent? To 80 percent?

3.6 Brainstorm some ways that you could start to increase the amount of time you spend on your high yield activities and reduce the amount of time you spend on your low-yield activities:

Saying Yes / Saying No

Is it difficult for *you* to say "no" to people when they request your time? (If you're not sure, ask your spouse or a close friend what they think.) If so, think about the people who ask for your time most often.

3.7 What do they ask you to fit into your schedule?

3.8 How do these activities measure up to your high-yield activities?

3.9 What is the worst thing that could happen with each person if you started to say "no" to half of their requests?

3.10 Would there be a way for you to "transfer" their requests to an employee to handle?

Tame the Information Tiger

3.11 How would you describe your "state of mind" (or "quality of mind") when you start off your day?

3.12 List some ways that you get inundated with information:

3.13 Circle or highlight any of the sources of information above that are the most stressful for you.

3.14 Brainstorm some ways that you can reduce the amount of information coming at you for each of the circled or highlighted items.

Conquer Clutter

3.15 Describe your office or work area in terms of how organized it is:

3.16 List your "to do" list below for sorting through the paper clutter in your work area, according to the instructions in the chapter.

3.17 List your "to do" list below for sorting through clutter other than paper in your work area, according to the instructions in the chapter.

Good Habits / Bad Habits

3.18 After reading through the "*Habits*" section in the
chapter, what are some of your bad habits
you've become accustomed to?

3.19 What might you do to stop each of those habits?

3.20 What are some good habits you prefer to make
part of your regular way of doing business?

3.21 How might you begin to put into practice each of
these good habits?

The "Three Day" Plan

3.22 How can you start to create a half day each week as a half-Focus day?

3.23 When can you start to implement that change?

3.24 How can you then stretch the amount of time of your Focus day to one full day per week?

3.25 When will you aim to have one full Focus day per week?

3.26 How soon do you believe you can have two full Focus days per week?

3.27 How are you going to schedule your Free days?

Change Your Thinking

3.28 Are you a Futuristic thinker, Big-Picture thinker, Strategic thinker, or Current thinker?

3.30 What are your strengths as that type of thinker?

3.31 What are you weaknesses as that type of thinker?

3.32 Which other ways of thinking would be helpful for you to look into (and stretch) in order to be a more effective entrepreneur?

3.33 How would "thinking vertically" (which means "thinking deeper") help you to be more effective?

3.34 How would "thinking horizontally" (which means "thinking of more possibilities at the same level") help you to be more effective?

Set Goals

3.35 Set goals to reduce or eliminate these activities based on what you have written:

In the next month, I will...

For example, "In the next month, I will conduct phone interviews with three to five computer experts to help with our PCs, and by the end of the fourth week I will select one of them to work with our company."

In the next six months, I will...

In the next six to 12 months, I will...

Craft Your Business Structure & Systems

"I do not believe you can do today's job with yesterday's methods and be in business tomorrow."

—Nelson Jackson

*I*n order to survive and thrive, a business needs to have a structure to it, much like a house needs structure in terms of a foundation, frame, and walls so that people can live in the house. A business also needs to have systems created that actually run the business, just as a house needs a plumbing system and an electrical system to make it livable.

By having a structure—and systems within it—your business is much more likely to run smoothly. Have you ever visited a business (as a customer) and wondered how they ever make any money because their employees seem disorganized, uninformed, or incompetent? That business probably has poor structure, lack of good systems, or both. The staff doesn't know who reports to whom, how to resolve problems quickly (and to the satisfaction of customers), nor how to work well with each other as if the business is a well-oiled machine. When your business has a solid structure and systems that run properly, you can even get away from the business for a while without it falling apart.

Your Business Structure

An organization chart is a structure, so to speak, of your business. It maps out the major lines of responsibility, including who holds certain responsibilities and who reports to whom.

Do you know what your organization chart looks like? Do people understand their roles? Does your organizational structure support delivering a great product or service? If so, why? If not, why not? How can it be changed?

Jim, Jeff, and John are three brothers who own a small manufacturing business. When they realized they needed an organizational chart, they sat down together with paper and a pencil and started to draw it out. First they wrote a chart with titles, without entering anyone's name. It looked something like this:

"J" Company

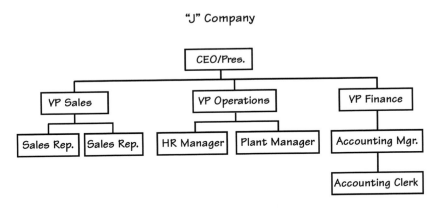

You need to create an organization structure, starting off by using the three basic departments (or divisions) of sales, operations, and finance, even if there are only a couple of you involved in your business. Other departments, such as research & development, marketing, and purchasing are usually subsets of the three main areas. In fact, every other function can pretty much be rolled into one of these three.

In a company so small that the owner has only one employee—himself—he performs all the roles. With a company that has several owners, each person may wear more than one hat on a given day. As the company gets bigger and more employees are hired, the new people may be asked to function in more than one capacity because no one job takes up the whole day or because there isn't a large enough budget to hire more people. However, with large companies, each employee tends to have more of a singularly defined role. So the bigger the company becomes, the more important it is to have a clear, and constantly updated, organization chart so that people know who to report to and what their own responsibilities are, and so that their job doesn't overlap with someone else's.

It must be kept in mind that in the early days of a business, people tend to gravitate to the jobs they love. The jobs they don't want—and, in fact, nobody wants—tend to be set aside and overlooked. The organizational chart makes it clear who is responsible for getting a particular job done whether the person wants to do it or not. If something begins to go wrong in that area, everyone knows who to go to.

Use your journal or the exercise in the Application section to sketch out an organization chart for your business. Are there any particular areas of your business that are unusual or unique which require their own section on the chart? Write it out as best as you can, tweaking the earlier example for "J" company to fit your business.

In our example of the brothers, Jim, Jeff, and John, after writing out their organization chart, they slotted names into the various roles and responsibilities, writing them directly onto the chart. Each of them took on numerous roles in the early days of their business until they were in a position to hire people. The chart gave them a clear picture of "who does what" and kept them from crossing each other. Jim was both the president and the vice-president of sales. Jeff was the vice-president of operations. And John was the vice-president of finance. In the early days of their business, Jim was selling for the company, in effect making him also a sales representative. John handled all of the banking relationships and accounting functions, which didn't take up too much of his time in the early days, so he also helped out Jeff in the operations of the business. After some time, they hired employees, and then settled back into their leadership roles, with Jim still being the president and the vice president of sales.

If your company has just a few people, each person will take on multiple roles. Make certain that the roles taken by one person are not conflicting (talk with your accountant about what types of roles would be conflicting roles for one person to perform). For a fairly new business, it is fine if someone is assigned a role or two that are not a perfect fit for who they are, what they want to do, and their particular strengths. It's nice if you can initially slot people into roles that exactly match their skill set, but in the beginning, some of you may need to fill roles that are not in line with your strengths. That can be changed as the business grows and more people are added to the organization.

Once you have created the organizational chart, plug in the names of people who will carry out the responsibilities of each role. This will include the vice presidents of major areas and perhaps managers of the areas reporting to each vice president. In a later chapter, *"Delegate to Generate More Success,"* you'll learn about delegating some tasks by outsourcing (rather than using employees). You can always come back to the organization chart and write in peoples' names (employees or outsourced vendors). Hey! Write it in pencil! Things change!

Once you've figured out the structure of your business, it's time to consider the various systems that run the business.

Your Business Systems

Every business, no matter how big or how small, has to use some kind of operating system, simply because every company is composed of several functioning parts that have to work together. You are producing either a product or a service, so you have to get out there and sell it somehow. You have to collect money from your customers. You have to interface with those customers in case there's a problem. You have to keep track of the financial records. Someone has to pay the utility bills to keep the lights and heat on. Someone has to keep an eye on employees to make sure they know what they're doing. And the list goes on.

Systems are not static. They are the conduit through which data, information, communication, money, products, and services can flow. In a business, it is an assemblage or a combination of parts that work together to keep the whole place running. Typically, systems are made up of separate departments, which function independently of each other and yet also interdependently. Each department is defined by its function, not by the person in charge of it. The organization chart, as you have seen, makes it clear just what that function is.

A system is like a machine, and a machine needs oil to operate smoothly. For a business to run like a well-oiled machine, the people in each of the departments have to know why it exists, what it is supposed to do, how it is supposed to do it, and each person's role in making it work. Basically, the people run the systems, and the systems run the business.

To help your people learn these things and apply that knowledge every day to their work, you need to provide them with training. The best type of training will not only give them information, but will also get it into their minds so that practicing what they learned is as easy as breathing.

If you schedule your people into a classroom setting with an instructor and well-written materials, you will provide them with the best opportunity to learn your systems and apply what they learned to their jobs every day. If you simply tell your employees what you want them to do and then expect them to remember it and run the business' systems, you may be sorely disappointed later when you find your people constantly making mistakes.

If you want your employees to run the business systems, you need to start with a set of written materials, such as training manuals, that they can follow. Introducing people to the documentation in a classroom setting will enhance their learning retention.

Typically, the areas of a business that need to be documented are sales, operations, marketing, accounting, accounts receivable, accounts payable, purchasing, employee policies, computer usage, employee training, and customer service.

When these types of topics are documented into manuals in a "how to" fashion, employees can more easily follow them and stay consistent when they run the business systems. Without documented systems, a company runs the risk of creating gaping holes in the business and important tasks may be ignored.

Why can't a company develop its systems for doing business without creating documentation of the systems? Because we humans are forgetful and, while we think we remember the original pattern for doing any activity, we don't always recall the details. Going back to the original is always best.

Think about it this way: When you need to make copies of your house key, it is best to copy the original key. Have you ever made a key from a copy (either because you couldn't find the original or because a copy was handy)? I've done that. The new key didn't open the door!

Here is another illustration: When I was a girl, a lot of my friends and I sewed our own clothes. We sewed craft projects, too, and sometimes made our own patterns. For some craft projects, we needed to cut many pieces of fabric the same size. One time I remember we used a pattern to cut the first piece, then used the first piece to cut the second piece, used the second piece to cut the third piece, and so on. By the time we cut the seventh piece of fabric, it didn't match all of the others! We should have used the pattern to cut all of the fabric.

Likewise, by documenting your business systems, you ensure that you and your employees follow a pattern that can be repeated. This creates consistency that your employees can follow, even in unusual circumstances. It also ensures that your customers will be treated with a consistent high level of service.

Have you ever been a customer of a business that seemed to treat you inconsistently? It's disconcerting! One time you get one response; the next time you get a completely different answer. When you are in that type of situation as a client, how do you feel? Like you've brought your business to people who are incompetent, right? And then you begin to think about your alternatives, such as bringing your business elsewhere!

In the past week I've spoken to three people who travel for business frequently, one of whom works with several people who travel every week. Each of them told me that they and their co-workers have switched their loyalty to a different airline because the company they were flying became inadequate at customer service. The biggest complaint was the inconsistency in the airline's response to customers and their representatives' lack of knowledge. All of this was due to the lack of excellent systems, the lack of well-documented systems, not following the systems that were already in place, or a combination.

Having excellent documented systems in place flushes out ambiguity and ensures consistency. Your customers will be the first to notice whether you have systems in place or not. Your employees may recognize that fact *after* your customers have already figured it out.

I'm a believer in well-written documentation: user manuals, training manuals, policy manuals, etc., and a good training plan to back it up. There is no substitute for employees who are well-trained in their company's systems, who not only understand what they learned in a training class, but who can reference materials later to answer questions. Well-trained employees can also apply what they learn to a new situation that is not specifically covered in the documentation, and arrive at a great solution.

A friend of mine was consulting with a large company. This business practically wrote the book on creating systems that run their business. They are a fast food company that, for many years, has continued to develop and improve upon teamwork and creating systems that run the business. At this company, they created systems that run everything from the point the customer arrives (at the door or at the drive-up window) to quick service of the food, of a quality their customers expect. Their "systems" have been taught to employees for many years to ensure fast service of the same quality of food in all of their restaurants. Their systems ensure that customers receive the same products and service at every restaurant all over the world.

When I spoke with this friend, however, she was frustrated with the employees' mentalities, which she described robotically as, "This is how we make a French fry. This is how we make a hamburger." When she recited those sentences, she literally acted out the whole scene, looking like a spaced-out robot. Her point was that their systems were so ingrained in the employees that they could not envision any other way of doing business.

The benefits of creating systems that run the business are consistency and reliability. When your employees have a system to run the business, you, the owner, can actually get away from the business to develop more sales, do research, or take time off. The downside of having systems that run the business occurs when employees use the systems to the point of ignoring innovation. When you create your systems, keep in mind that you never drop innovation. As you run your business with systems (which are, in turn, run by your employees), keep innovating concurrently. As you come up with new ways of doing things, implement your new plans and replace existing systems, either in part or in whole.

Part of designing a system involves educating employees. Your employees run the system while the system runs the business. Training employees well is key to a system's success. This includes training people beyond simply performing like androids, and helping them to learn to be innovative, using all of their skills, and applying their skills to problem-solving as they run the system. (We will cover this further in a later chapter, "*Lead Great Teams.*")

Sum it Up

Before leaving this chapter, work through some thoughts to apply the ideas of *structure* and *systems* to your business. Use your journal and follow the steps in the Application section to put a structure and systems in place or to enhance what you have already established.

****

Next, if you ever wondered how you can possibly compete with big businesses in your particular industry, your stellar customer service is the one thing that will keep customers coming back. In the next chapter, you will figure out what "wows" your customers and how to create good experiences for them over and over.

Application

Your Business Structure

In *Catapult*, I suggest that you sketch out an organizational chart early-on to get your thoughts moving in the direction of creating a structure for your business. Below is a shell of a chart where you can slot in names of people who will perform the particular roles. Use a pencil to write them in, as peoples' roles change over time. Keep in mind that in the earlier days of a business, people will often perform multiple roles, the lower levels of the chart will often be unnamed (because a few people are doing all of the work, and, as you use outsourced services to provide several services for your business, the names of the people or businesses to whom the work is outsourced may appear on your organizational chart).

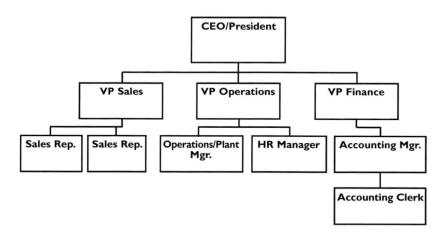

As the company grows, add more roles to your organizational chart and fill in the appropriate names and titles for the people who fill those roles. An org chart with more roles in a small business might look like this:

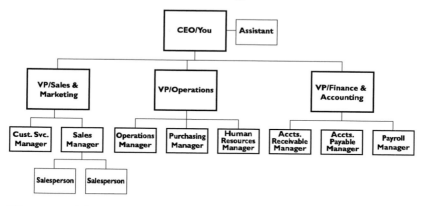

Now consider this:

- How can you best communicate to every employee and business partner (basically everyone except for certain outsourced people) how your organizational chart appears, who reports to whom, who is responsible for what, and how communication should flow?

- How do you envision your organizational chart to look in five years?

- In 10 years?

Your Business Systems

When a house is built, its foundation, frame, walls, and roof make up its structure. Then, once that is in place, the systems inside it (such as the plumbing system and electrical system) make it possible for people to live in it. Today we might even consider the communications systems inside a house (such as telephone, cable/broadband, and wireless systems) to be necessary to make the house livable.

Much like a house needs the systems inside it in order to be inhabitable, a business needs its systems in order to run well and make a profit. Without systems that run really well, a business can falter, lose money, and close.

As mentioned in the chapter, building systems in your business (and the documentation to support it), helps your business to run smoothly and even run without you! Consider the following questions for each of the areas that are numbered on the next page.

Which of these are already "up and running" in your business?

Which will be busier in the next three to five years?

Write next to each *what is going on in that area.*

Are you doing all of the work for that area?

How is that working for you?

Is that area taking your time away from more important tasks that could bring in more money?

Do you have any documentation regarding how to run that particular area?

4.1 Sales

4.2 Operations

4.3 Marketing

4.4 Accounting

4.5 Accounts Receivable

4.6 Accounts Payable

4.7 Purchasing

4.8 Employee Policies

4.9 Computer Usage

4.10 Employee Training

4.11 Customer Service

4.12 Other: _____

4.13 Other: _____

Next, consider for which of the areas above you will most likely have employees in the next one to three years. How can you develop a step-by-step guide for how to run that particular area of your business?

How can you then train someone to run that area without much supervision from yourself?

Create Superb Customer Service

"Profit in business comes from repeat customers; customers who boast about your product or service, and that brings friends with them."

—W. Edwards Demming

*P*aula Begoun is the president of a skincare and cosmetics company called Paula's Choice. Before becoming an entrepreneur, she had been a make up artist, salesperson, and consumer reporter for the cosmetics and skincare industry (she calls herself the "cosmetics cop"). She had also written books informing and enlightening consumers about the skin care and cosmetics industries. Finally, she started a skincare and cosmetics company, fashioning her product line in keeping with the lessons she learned. She kept costs reasonable and offered the type of customer service she herself wished for when she was on the other side of the counter. Since her products are sold through her catalog and online, people could order directly. Though I have never met Paula, I have been a loyal customer of her product line for years. On one occasion, I had trouble with a particular item and had to send it back. They replaced it, but I had to send that one back also. Finally, I asked for a refund, which they cheerfully gave me. All was well; I expected nothing more. Yet after a brief period, I received a letter that was signed by Paula herself (I could tell from the quick, presidential script) apologizing for the problem. She then did the unthinkable: She told me about three products from competing companies that she thought would work for me. Wow! A prompt refund, itself, is welcome enough, but a personal apology letter with helpful product suggestions that can't possibly benefit her company— that was exceptional. Am I a customer for life? *Absolutely*.

As a business owner, your agenda is simple: You want as many people as possible to buy from you and not from a competitor. *Simple*? Yes. *Easy*? No. You have to make your company stand out from the rest, giving your customers a compelling reason to come back to you over and over rather than go to someone else. What can you offer that keeps people coming back and convinces them to pass your name on to others? There must be something that makes yours stand out from the competition in a positive way.

As we can see from the opening example, the key feature you can offer is excellent customer service—service that makes your customers say, "Wow!" This is the area of your business that interfaces with the public (and other businesses) and deals with their needs. The whole process is usually initiated by the customer when he contacts you to get questions answered, issues discussed, and problems resolved. The usual belief is that this area of doing business is rather joyless and consists only of listening to people gripe about something. However, if you are proactive about it and take steps to create a positive experience, you will have fewer grumpy customers to deal with, you'll spend far less time chasing down solutions to problems that never should have occurred in the first place, and you'll have loyal customers.

Never forget that your goal isn't just to attract new customers but to keep the old ones coming back over and over—and for them to bring their friends! Today, customer service is considered part of marketing: It's not just about problem solving anymore. This process actually helps position your business. You can become known as the "place that helps." Nordstrom department store is a good example. It has a huge following of customers who could buy at other department stores, but who keep coming back because they are treated so well and because the return policy is so good.

In this day and age, it is not enough to have a system in place for dealing with customers' issues promptly and smoothly. Now, you need a strategy with built-in extras, benefits that are above and beyond what the public expects from you and your business. These extras have to be planned into your regular, day-to-day commerce because you can be sure that your competitors are hanging out their own honeycomb trying to attract the same bees as you.

My brother knew a man named Jimmy who had his own tattoo shop. One year, at a trade show for the public, Jimmy was buried amidst hundreds of other tattoo artists who all seemed to offer the same service. Booths were set up from one end of the building to the other and they were all competing for the same customers. In this particular business, one thing Jimmy knew was that the people who work in the tattoo industry tended to be gruff and a little rough around the edges. He could see that this was a problem for people who were shopping around and had never had a tattoo before because there is always some fear that comes with getting the first one. A stranger is drilling a needle into your arm, and whatever words or picture you decide on lasts forever. This is bound to create some hesitation, so Jimmy thought a little TLC ("tender loving care") seemed to be in order for potential tattoo customers. To differentiate himself from the others in the industry at this trade show, Jimmy decided that his marketing strategy would be to smile and say hello to everyone walking by the booth. He had two employees at his booth and he enlisted them to do the same. "Let's be the un-scary tattoo artists," he said. Before long, they had a line of customers waiting to have a rose with the word *MOM* over it tattooed on their arm, whereas the booths all around his were begging for work.

Why did Jimmy's strategy work? Because of how he made his customers *feel.* People felt a lot better about stepping into his booth once they knew it would be safe and friendly. By signaling to people that they would have a positive experience if they came to him, he made it easy for them to overcome their fears and take the plunge. No one else was doing this, so he managed to differentiate his service from his competitors; none of them were concerned about how customers felt. He created an environment where people knew they were welcome and would be treated in a sincere and non-pushy way. Meanwhile, Brutus, the biker-guy next to him with the spiked leather jacket and the three-day growth of beard, sat there all day with little to do.

Today, there is so little civility in the world and so little emphasis on simple good manners and service that it stands out when you treat others politely. Most people have learned to be satisfied with even a modicum of this kind of treatment from the customer service department. When they've been paid a minimum of respect, at least they don't go away mad. But is that enough? You haven't kept them away, yet you haven't made sure they're coming back either. When your customer service is superb, however, it seals the deal. People walk out the door thinking, "I've hardly ever been treated this well. I feel like royalty." This is the kind of feeling that inspires loyalty.

When is the last time you had an experience with a company that left you saying "Wow!" What did they do that led you to respond that way?

Here are just a few examples of businesses that provoked a "Wow!" from their customers:

- The distribution center whose customer service staff takes the initiative to call people back and follow up on their problems rather than wait to be called.
- The dentist whose staff offers a hot washcloth to patients after treatment.
- The car wash that serves flavored coffee and real cream in a clean, comfortable waiting room.
- The auto-body shop that returns cars to the owners, not only repaired but cleaned inside and out, and the tires shined with Armour All.
- The consulting firm that meets client expectations for quality work that's delivered on time, and is agreeable to adjust invoices for any end-product delivered late.

The greatest results about eliciting a "Wow!" response is that the person remembers you, you get a customer for life, and they tell their friends and acquaintances about you. Isn't it worth the extra effort to gather these benefits?

Create the "Wow!"

So how do you create this type of incredible customer loyalty? It starts with several character traits that you make a point of incorporating into your customer service practices. It all starts with you, the owner. You have to embody all the traits you want your employees to possess. If you are rude, demanding, and ill-mannered, that is going to set the tone for everyone else. The managers have to practice them also, followed by the rest of the employees. In other words, everyone has to hop on board so that good service and good manners trickle down to the customer. If you want to get employees on board and train them to treat people well, then it's important how you treat them. The same positive traits you display towards them will be evident when they're dealing with the paying public.

It isn't just the employees who directly interface with the public who count. In a way, the tone of the whole business matters. If you train people without any sense of respect and the general business practice is for management to swear at people and yell at them whenever something goes wrong, one way or another, that is going to trickle down to the customer. You need to work on instilling good character traits into your employees and teaching them that they represent the face of the company whenever and however they interface with the public. One sour employee can poorly color a customer's impression of your entire business.

Remember that each positive character trait *practiced* will create the right feeling in your customers—that of being welcomed, respected, valued and appreciated—which will keep them coming back for more. They will remember how you made them feel about themselves more than they'll remember the employees' faces or amount of time spent or the product or services involved in the incident. Think about the memorable incidents in your life. Isn't that what you always walk away with? How did the person make you feel about yourself?

Sincerity

Given that the marketplace is not known for sincerity, it is remarkable how important sincerity is to the process of doing business. It is crucial because it makes your customers feel seen, heard, acknowledged, and understood. When you show this important trait, the people who walk into your office or store will never think they're being pushed around or forced into making a decision. Rather, they will believe that their feelings and needs are being heard and taken into account. Once a customer feels seen, heard, acknowledged, and understood, she is more likely to come back to your business again and again.

Some of you are probably thinking, "Sincerity. Yeah, I can fake that." Not really. People can always tell when someone is laying it on thick and doesn't mean a word he says. Even if sincerity isn't your strongest natural trait, you can conjure it up by keeping in mind that these customers are paying your mortgage and putting your kids through college. That, alone, should bring up warm feelings for them.

I have also known people who were sincere, but they were sincerely awful. They were aggressive, pushy, and selfish, and they didn't hide it. A wise person once said, "The worst thing you can tell some people is to *be yourself*," because, when they are, unfortunately, they're being selfish, snappy, and churlish. It's not enough to be genuine and sincere if you don't have a few other positive traits to offer as well.

Trustworthiness

It's true that in this day and age, con men who are heads of corporations are on the front page of the newspapers daily. Corruption is certainly part of the fabric of the business world, sometimes on a small scale and sometimes on a large scale. But sooner or later, your customers will catch on. It is far better for your business to aspire to trustworthiness through a policy of honesty than to cut corners and make a few extra dollars here and there by cheating people. When a person knows you can be trusted, he feels confident about returning to you for years to come. He doesn't have to question you or wonder if he will be treated fairly. This kind of trust makes it easier to take the leap and come to you for the big ticket items or the important contract. In the long run, honesty always pays off.

Think back over your own history of when you were the customer. Did you ever sense a little red flag waving, a warning bell ringing in your head? We all have a built-in alert system that makes us aware that something is off, that we need to keep our guard up, that we need to watch this transaction carefully because something isn't right. This red flag is a precursor to fear. It is telling you that if you don't change course, you will find yourself in deep water. Remember the fight or flight lesson you probably heard about in a psychology class? This is the body's way of telling you to run away. Some of us listen to it and some of us don't. When we don't, we come to regret it afterwards. In business, the red flag is usually warning us that the person on the other side of the desk or counter cannot be trusted. What are some examples of "the little red flag" feeling?

- The salesman tells you that the product can do X, Y and Z and then fly to the moon. When he is asked to demonstrate these functions, however, he finds some excuse not to.
- There is no warranty or guarantee available with the sale.
- The salesperson sighs and makes excuses when you ask him additional questions or request more information.
- As the customer service rep (CSR) speaks to you, she leaves the words, "you idiot" off the end of her last sentence, but she may as well have included them.
- The CSR raises his voice when you question his claims, especially since they seem like they're out of the ballpark.
- The smooth-talking car salesman tries to charm the pants off of you and convince you how much fun it would be to drive the car home off the lot right away. "Don't go home and think it over. The car might be gone when you come back." (Whenever someone tells you *not* to think about a purchase, your red flag should start waving like something caught in a hurricane.)
- You're searching for a new computer and the salesperson is bombarding you with technical information you've already said you don't understand.

He's hoping you will end the embarrassing confusion
by signing on the dotted line. The problem is, you
might be purchasing a lot more options than you need.

Respect

Treating people with respect is much easier if you're selling them socks or baseball hats. It's a straightforward deal
and there's not a lot to explain. If you are selling them a high-
tech item or even a major appliance with lots of bells and
whistles, though, offering respect can be more challenging.
Most customers don't know as much about what array of
products are out there and may not even really know what
they need. You have to spend more time explaining and even
teaching. They might ask quite a few naïve questions about
why your product costs so much more than the one across
town, when you know perfectly well that there is no comparison
in terms of quality. Because they don't understand what they're
dealing with, customers cannot always accurately evaluate
why yours is still a better deal even though it costs more.

Senior citizens and people who neither speak nor
understand English well also pose a challenge. In addition,
it is well documented that with certain products—like
automobiles and power tools—male clerks tend to be
dismissive of women. They think they can put one over on
"the fairer sex" because women either don't understand the
market or they don't know how to bargain. All of these people
may need more assistance than others. Because ours is a
society that respects and recognizes youth and people who
are "just like us," we often have to work extra hard to give
respect to those who are older or different.

If you believe you have respect for a customer, but you aren't actually showing it, your feelings will make little difference. Treating people with respect can take on a number of forms. Look them in the eye in a nonaggressive way. Listen fully to their questions before attempting an answer so that when you speak, they don't feel they've been cut off. Show a genuine interest in the questions they bring to the table using your tone of voice. A certain type of tone can suggest that you're being dismissive or belittling. For an older person, showing respect may involve explaining the kind of basic details most of the people you deal with already know. For someone from another country, it may involve repeating their questions back to them to make sure you understood them. For people who have very little money or are on a tight budget, showing respect might mean leading them through the costs, step by step, to demonstrate why your product or service will actually save them money.

Patience

Patience is a close cousin of respect, and in this era of computer time, it is a tall order. Studies show that people who used computers all the time (and who doesn't?) have developed unrealistic expectations of how long it should take a human being to respond to a question. To counter that tendency in yourself, you may have to train yourself to listen to a customer's issue, to wait until you're sure she has finished talking, and then to rephrase her issues or questions to let her know you're making an effort to give her the time and consideration she needs.

For example, after a customer finishes explaining what's

wrong with an appliance, you might try saying, "Mrs. Smith, if I hear you correctly, you're saying that the answering machine you purchased from us is supposed to give the caller ample chance to leave a message, allow you to screen all your calls, and hold the messages until you choose to delete them. Is that correct? It did all this for a while, and then it started cutting the caller off. Is that correct?" This shows that you heard every point she made, and it lets her add a point or change one if she wants to. When you're patient, you generously give the space to let complete communication take place. Don't be like the answering machine that cuts people off.

Both respect and patience are character traits that go hand in hand. People need to know that you're not judging them because they have a problem, that you hold them in high esteem, and that you deem it worthwhile to give them the time they need.

Helpfulness

The final trait I want to discuss is helpfulness, which means you are attentive to your customers' needs. This may seem like an obvious part of customer service, but unfortunately it isn't to everyone. This, of course, means that you first have to recognize their need, not interpret what they're saying in a way that is convenient to you. So being helpful requires you to first be patient and respectful. Then you are in a position to address their problem because you genuinely understand what the problem is.

Various ways of being helpful are:
  • having enough employees on hand to take care of
    everyone who walks in the door

- having a phone system in place that can actually be navigated
- indicating clearly on the phone greeting how customers can reach a real live person without pressing every number on the phone pad
- telling people exactly when an order will be filled in the case of an item not being in stock
- directing people to the aisle where their product is shelved
- making sure customers don't have to wait in line for a disagreeably long period of time
- selecting employees for the customer service department who are genuinely helpful by nature and who are fully informed about all kinds of customer issues.

Now let's consider the kinds of specific behaviors you can show that will put your customers at ease:

1. Keep your eyes on the person who is speaking to you. This is critical to helping her feel heard. But only make eye contact for as long as it is comfortable to do so. In the U.S., we can typically look a person directly in the eye for several seconds, then look away for a split second, and then look again. If you maintain continuous eye contact for minutes at a time, it is unnerving for most people. Different cultures have a different tolerance for this, so you might want to take your cue from the person you are in dialogue with. (By the way, there is a theory that if you really want a person to remember what you're saying, look into his right eye as you

speak and the message will likely go straight to the left brain [the side that processes information logically] and hence stick in his memory.)

2. Pay attention to body language. It expresses, silently, your attitude toward the person to whom you are speaking. For instance, when we find someone interesting, we tend to lean in toward him. Conversely, when we are bored, we tend to lean away. Without doing so consciously, most people can "read" the body signals being sent to them and are aware on some level of what the other person's true feelings are.

3. Other postures signal that the employee is competent, friendly, confident, and self-assured. People who are in this frame of mind naturally keep their head level, both horizontally and vertically. They tilt their head slightly to either side when they are interested in what's being said to them. Keep both of these postures in mind when interacting with customers. There are times when it's more important to be taken seriously. In this case, keep your head straight. When you want customers to think of you as open and friendly, tilt your head a little to the left or right.

4. When you are standing and talking with a customer, keep your arms at your sides, or have one or both behind your back. This tells the other person that you are open and receptive to her. You don't have to be frozen in your position however. You can use your arms and hands as you talk to avoid appearing

robotic. Just make sure your gestures aren't too grand and over the top or the listener will feel overwhelmed.

5. Try to refrain from folding your arms across your chest, which makes you appear self-protective or defensive. (If you're cold, put on another layer of clothing!) Also avoid holding a conversation with your hands on your hips, which can lead customers to feel defensive or think you're not open to him, regardless of how friendly your words are.

There are also some behaviors and ways of communicating that are considered objectionable, and you do not want them to be part of your customer service practices:

1. Don't be gruff when speaking.
2. Don't be defensive even when the customer is upset or angry. It's not personally against you.
3. Don't try to convince the person that the problem is his fault and not the company's fault.
4. Don't flip the question back at the customer by saying, "Well, what do you want us to do?" This kind of response is like a door slamming in his face. It's the kind of question that ends a conversation instead of opening one, and it makes the person feel as if you don't care and aren't going to help.
5. Don't say "no" outright to a request. That ends the transaction immediately. Instead, keep the doors open by saying, "Well, I can't do that, but I can do this." Keep the whole conversation on a positive note.
6. Don't mix up paperwork – such as misplacing a

check, an important contract, an agreement, or a warranty. It usually creates a lot of work for the customer who has to help you track it down and it makes him think you are incompetent.

7. If you are a solo professional operating by appointment only, and you can't make it on some occasion, don't miss a meeting without calling as far ahead of time as possible. And you should try not to miss one at all except when you are ill. With all the scheduling and communication tools available today, there is no excuse to miss deadlines or appointments as a result of forgetfulness.

Your Customer's Experience Today

Every customer who walks through your door or calls you on the phone is going to be left with an impression. It's up to you whether it's positive or negative. The experience the prospect or customer has determines whether she'll come back to do business with you again or whether she will go to your competitor. It also determines whether she will give you a glowing recommendation to other prospects. This is an advantage you can never underestimate.

The experience the customer has with your business is entirely in your hands. You have complete control over the situation, and you can keep people satisfied every time if you pay particular attention to how they are treated. When you listen to what they want and tend to their needs, they feel special, and that turns into free advertising when they tell other people about their good experience. In fact, you can't *buy* a good experience; all you can really do is *create* an experience so positive that the next time they want this product or service, they only think of you. You can spend all your additional advertising dollars to bring in new customers.

Let's look with a critical eye at what your customer's experience might be like now. What impression is he or she left with after dealing with your company? We're not reviewing what goes right with your service, but rather what does, or can, go wrong.

The Prospect Inquires

Is your employee impolite, curt, uninformed, or inattentive when a prospect first telephones or shows up at your business? If the contact is in person, is your employee slovenly, does he fail to make eye contact, is she finishing a personal call before tending to the customer, or is she not present at the front desk so the person has to wait?

If the contact is by phone, are they endlessly rerouted through your phone system before a real person (if ever) comes on the line? Are they put on hold and forgotten about until someone completely unfamiliar with the case accidentally presses the button and speaks to them? Are people routinely disconnected because employees don't know how to work the phones? Or is the customer sent to the wrong person, then cut off, then has to start all over again?

If most prospects find your business via the Internet, can they find contact information easily and quickly? Or do they need to click the mouse more than two times in order to find a phone number or e-mail form?

The First Sale

If your business sells products, various things can go wrong with the first sale. The item isn't in stock or the representative doesn't have authorization to make a decision on the spot. He cannot answer questions correctly, he quotes the wrong price, or he takes too long to find information or a product. He sells too hard or he doesn't care enough about selling anything. The employee lacks the skill to perform a task for the customer, or he makes amateur mistakes that should have been caught before they ever made it to this stage.

If your company provides a service, a number of mistakes might be made. A technician who is supposed to be at the person's house between 9 a.m. and 3 p.m. doesn't show up or call; the customer has just taken a day off work for nothing. The support for any type of electronic office equipment doesn't come with adequate instructions for making it work with the customer's existing equipment, but the tech support fails to listen fully to everything that will be expected of the product and everything else it will have to interface with. The customer brings it home, and nothing works.

The Customer Receives the Product or Service

In this scenario, we are talking about people ordering from catalogs or the Internet, businesses ordering from sales representatives, or someone requesting a service.

The customer has been overpromised on a product or service. The product arrives broken, or the wrong product is sent out and has to be returned. A technician shows up without the proper parts or is extremely late. He is young and extremely inexperienced; he makes mistakes and won't take responsibility for them. The product sent by the catalog arrives a week later than promised and the credit card holder is charged long before the item reaches him. The invoice is incorrect or missing. With insurance, tax, or financial services, the paperwork that arrives in the mail is incomprehensible to all sentient beings, and the client has no idea where to sign.

The Customer Has a Problem with the Product or Service

When the customer calls to resolve a problem, she is caught in a telephone loop and sent to every department in the company, with each one referring her to someone else. She is put on hold, and when an employee takes the call, he asks her to explain the problem all over again. The employee isn't in any position to make a final decision about the disposition of the case and doesn't know what to tell her to do next. He keeps offering unacceptable solutions, causing the customer to grow angrier and more frustrated. The representative gives the customer the runaround because he doesn't want to make good on a promise or correct his own mistakes. He is trying to handle the case way too quickly and doesn't listen long enough to find out what's really wrong. The customer complains about the quality of the previous contact with the company, and the representative sides with the employee and is unwilling to look into it. The customer has to call again and again to receive any kind of disposition of her case. She is deluged with red tape and not told what to do with it all. Or she is shuffled around from one employee to the next.

Follow-up Contact

Your company promises excellent follow-up support in their sales campaign and they don't come through. The customer is called back about the sale or the problem, but only after a long period of time. The follow-up is on time, but it fails to resolve the problem. The representative making the call has not contacted an employee with higher authority first, so he doesn't know what he can and cannot offer. The follow-up is conducted by the wrong person. The employee hasn't done his homework and the customer has to explain the problem all over again. The promises and commitments made during the follow-up call are not kept. The customer is charged for the call when it should be part of the service.

Future Sales

The customer returns after the first sale, which went very well, but now that the initial sale has been made, the staff is not very interested in her because your company is set up to pour all its energy, effort, and time into the initial contact and first sale. For the original salesperson, this is all he does, so he went out of his way to make the customer feel special. But the others have a lot on their plate, and the individual customer feels she is being put on the back burner. After the big first sale is made, you are underprepared to keep the customer happy in subsequent sales. The initial salesperson is out of the loop now, and the customer has to deal with customer service or sales assistants or operations people.

The customer is surprised that she has to spend even more money on follow-up just to get the original product to work for her company. Something went wrong in the first contact, but it was insignificant, and so it was forgiven by the customer; but by the fifth contact with the same mistake being made over and over, the mistake is beginning to wear on her. In the time between the original sale and the second contact, there has been personnel change, and the new people don't know what they're doing.

New and Improved Customer Service

Now let's discuss what each of these stages might look like *after* you have reviewed your customer service agenda and fixed the problems.

The Prospect Inquires

The prospect is greeted immediately upon entering so that he knows he is seen and welcomed. He calls and speaks with personnel immediately, someone who is eager to help. If the employee who is first contacted is not the right person for the job, she can quickly transfer the customer to the correct person without delay or confusion. What does the customer feel after this treatment? Like he is important and being taken care of, and his impression of your business is that everyone knows what they are doing, and that he is dealing with a well-run company.

The First Sale

Virtually all products are in stock, and if something is not, your employees know how to order it quickly and efficiently. They know which catalog to consult, which department to call, and which order form to fill out. There won't be any snags with ordering the wrong product and having to start all over. If your customer needs technical help, a well-trained technician is available, helpful, and friendly. Whatever the case, your employees are able to handle any customer issues swiftly and to the person's satisfaction.

The Customer Receives the Product or Service

Because the previous step was handled correctly, the customer receives what he asked for in a timely way. The product works properly, all the parts that are supposed to come in the box are actually in the box, and none of them are broken. "How-to" manuals are in plain English, not mangled English. All services rendered are in keeping with the customer's reasonable expectations.

The Customer Returns for a Problem with the Product or Service

Even if the other steps went well, problems can always crop up once the customer either takes the product home or receives the service. The problem might not even be your company's fault. Nevertheless, it is up to you to provide a solution. One important point to make clear to your employees is not to get into an unwinnable argument about who was right and who was wrong. If the customer's expectations are unreasonable, you might respectfully point out that this is how things are done in this business. Take it out of the personal realm and explain your policy objectively. That way, they don't think they're being singled out for poor treatment. It's just policy.

Follow-up Contact

Your company doesn't wait for the customer to call back to find out whether you have a solution to his problem, whether you have found his missing product, or whether you have the information he requested. Your people are on top of it, and they call him back. He doesn't have to chase you down, which tells him that he is valuable to you and that your company is efficient enough to keep track of his case.

Future Sales to the Customer

You do want to stay in touch to keep your company's name in the customer's mind so when they want this product or service again, they return to you. However, there's a fine line between that and making the customer feel badgered with junk mail, excessive email solicitations, or phone calls. Pestering people will keep you in their mind in ways that you don't want. Each industry has its own protocol for how often to stay in touch with the customer, and if you're not sure what that is, do a little research and you'll find out quickly. If you stay within this protocol, the customer won't be annoyed with you *and* you are more likely to make another sale.

What's Your "Wow"?

In an increasingly depersonalized world, you can be the company that's still nice to people. Wouldn't you like to be thought of in that way? Better yet, wouldn't you like to be the business that customers return to (and spend money at) for years into the future? Would it bring you satisfaction if you knew that your customers happily refer you to everyone they know?

Besides the outstanding products or services you sell, your *customer service* can be the area that most distinguishes you from your competitors because so many businesses overlook this important function. If you can make your customer service department shine, you will beat your competition every time.

Giving your customers the kind of service that will impress them must begin as soon as they walk in the door and it never ends as long as they need what you have to offer. You, as the owner, set the tone in your company regarding how you believe people should be treated. Your employees will learn through your behavior, and this attitude trickles down to how customers are treated. If you extend respect and consideration to everyone who works for you, they will turn around and give the same to those who come to do business with you. *"Treat people like royalty; it comes back to you in loyalty."*

Don't just sit back and wait for someone to complain about your service before you improve it. By then, you will have probably lost a customer, and you have certainly lost referrals. People never rave about a place once they have something to complain about. They only rave when they are gratified and content throughout their entire dealing with your business. In other words, they applaud you when you exceed their expectations. So be proactive. How can you make your customers say, "Wow!"?

Sum it Up

This chapter has given you a lot to think about regarding creating customer loyalty. What kinds of thoughts have gone through your mind related to your business? Use your journal and the steps in the Application section to capture your ideas and apply them to your business.

****

Meanwhile, do you ever comically wonder how you can clone yourself so that you can accomplish everything on your schedule? I feel your pain! The next chapter helps you identify when and how to delegate tasks.

Application

Getting the *"Wow!"* That is the response you want from your customers. You want them to be so happy about their experience with your business that they actually say, "Wow!" (They may also *think* "Wow!" rather than say it out loud! Thinking it is just as good as saying it.)

Once a customer says "Wow!" about the great service they received from a business, they usually become very loyal customers. They are unlikely to switch to a competitor. They refer new people to the business. Even if someone at the company makes a mistake in their regard, they are likely to easily forgive.

You've read about several businesses and how they got the "Wow!" response out of their customers. Did you have any thoughts about how you might get the "Wow!" from your own customers?

5.1 What does your business sell?

5.2 Thinking as if you are one of your customers, consider what they expect from your business in terms of the sales process and customer service. Describe what they expect from your business *at minimum*:

5.3 Describe what your customers expect from your business that would make them think, "That was good" (but not necessarily a "Wow! That was great!")

Go back to page 103 and read the bulleted list that other businesses have done to get the "Wow!"

List some ideas about what your business might do for customers, either during the sales process or through other customer service opportunities, in order to get the "Wow!"	How could you implement the idea? How much work would it take? How much would it cost?

5.4 Which of the ideas listed previously can you do before the others? (Choose one, two, or three.) What is it going to take for you to actually start doing those?

For each of the following traits, rate on a scale of 1 to 10 (with 10 being the best) how well you believe you and your employees model that trait in the eyes of your customers. Then, in the column on the right, state why you believe your customers would rate your people at that number:

Trait	Rate 1 to 10	Why would your customers rate your people in that manner?
Sincerity		
Trustworthiness		
Respect		
Patience		
Helpfulness		

For any of the traits for which you did not score a 10, list them below:	Brainstorm how your business could improve on each trait listed. (How would a customer feel and believe that you are being sincere, trustworthy, respectful, patient, and/or helpful?)

Take some time to think about how you want your customers to experience your business. What if they always had a great experience? Describe on the next page what each scenario would look like in your business' "best practices."

5.5 Your prospect inquires about your product or service:

5.6 A new customer buys for the first time:

5.7 Your new customer receives their product or service:

5.8 Your customer returns (or calls) about a problem regarding the product or service:

5.9 Someone at your business contacts the customer to follow-up (either after a sale or after a customer service inquiry):

5.10 The customer returns to buy more:

How can you start to implement your "best practices?"

Delegate to Generate More Success

"Surround yourself with the best people you can find, delegate authority, and don't interfere."

—Ronald Reagan

Kevin is a fun-loving, outgoing entrepreneur who owns a business in distribution of small parts. He has five employees who handle the office and additional employees who work in the warehouse. When I met him, he said that from the time he started the business 10 years earlier until just one year prior, he had taken care of all activities related to sales to new and existing customers, building customer relationships, keeping technology current, analyzing financial statements, collections, and handling customer issues. At that time, he said he realized that, in order for the business to grow and for him to have a more balanced life, he needed to give some of his responsibilities to other people. He knew this would mean giving some duties to existing employees, hiring new people, or outsourcing the work.

Kevin disliked handling collections, so he chose to give that duty to an employee who worked with accounts receivable. He thought this was a better idea than outsourcing collections and, because their aging reports were not too bad, it seemed like a good fiscal alternative. The employee chosen for the task is determined and yet fairly quiet. Kevin thought she would be a perfect fit for collections because of her resolve and because she already worked with accounts receivable and was familiar with outstanding balances. He decided to also give her the responsibility of handling customer issues.

Staying current with technology seemed to take up more time than he desired, so Kevin chose to look into outsourcing that responsibility to a firm in the area that would help him keep the computers and software up to date. After getting several referrals, meeting with potential vendors, and reviewing their proposals, he selected a company to take over that task.

When starting a business, an entrepreneur finds himself performing many tasks. Some of these tasks will be easy for him to perform and will come quite naturally. Other tasks will be more difficult and not his forté. For example, an entrepreneur who is a creative type of person will find product development to be easy, but may find handling the paperwork and financial matters to be a struggle. Likewise, an entrepreneur who is analytical will find setting up and running the computer system and interpreting business data to be easy tasks, while marketing and sales tasks may take a lot out of him. Since extra money is usually scarce in the beginning of a new venture, business owners will find themselves doing activities for the business that they will not have to always perform. As a business grows, owners need to delegate tasks to others in order to sustain, and not stunt, growth. Each time a little extra money becomes available, owners need to examine which tasks they can turn over to other people.

Some owners continue to perform tasks for years that should have been delegated to others much earlier. If an owner chooses to keep doing many tasks herself, her time will not be freed up for her to focus on the activities for her business that bring her the most bang for her buck. Instead, time will be taken away from the activities that yield her the most money (in the short-term and long-term) and given to tasks that don't yield much (or any) money. (But you remember that from an earlier chapter, right?)

By delegating tasks to others, an owner frees her time for the most important, high-yield activities of the business (plus, delegating tasks to others will give her some free time to spend outside of the business).

In order to delegate tasks, an owner has several choices. He can give tasks to an existing employee. He can hire a new employee to take on delegated tasks. Or he can use an outside business to take on the task (which is called "outsourcing").

What types of tasks should the owner delegate? First, she needs to determine all of the tasks she currently performs for her business. After compiling her list of current tasks, the owner reviews it and notes, first, whether the task is something she does well (a *strength*) or not very well (a *weakness*). Next, for the tasks she performs well, she notes which of those are better handled by someone else because it doesn't yield much money for the business. (She might be a whiz at cleaning the office, but she can pay someone a reasonable sum to clean it for her.) Last, of the remaining *strength tasks*, she reviews each to determine if those tasks, indeed, bring a monetary, high-yield value to the business (either in direct, immediate sales, or in reaching long-term goals, such as involvement in future product or service development to keep current and to keep product/service offerings fresh). For those tasks that bring (or that will bring in the future) a fairly high yield to the business, the owner can keep doing those tasks for the time being.

Now the owner goes back to the list of her tasks that she identified as her *weaknesses*. If the list is short, she may be able to hand those tasks over to other people fairly quickly. If the list is long, she will have to prioritize the list based on two factors: 1) *How important is it that this task be removed from me soon?* 2) *How quickly can I find someone to take over this task?* The "sooner/quicker" responses to those two questions will determine which tasks she should focus on delegating first in order to get them off her plate as soon as possible.

When delegating tasks, it's important to choose people with some careful thought. Consider what you want them to do and the types of skills, experience, and personality required to perform that task well. What are the minimum "must-have" qualities you are looking for? Beyond the minimum, what other qualities would you like the person to have? After creating a list of *minimum* qualities and *beyond-minimum* qualities, it's time to decide who to interview for the position. When choosing people to interview, don't interview anyone who does not have the minimum, must-have qualities.

Your type of business will determine the method you use for finding qualified people. For many positions you can use the Internet, on sites such as Monster.com, to find people who have posted their resumes. There are also sites available for executive-level positions. If your business is fairly small, the position you want to fill is clerical, or the business is in a small-town area, using the local newspaper to place a classified ad can work well. Another method for finding great people locally is through networking with other business people you trust. And if you need to find people for outsourcing and the type of work doesn't require them to be local (i.e. certain types of writing, PowerPoint presentations, etc.), there are Internet sites such as Elance.com where you can find freelancers, or you can find a virtual assistant through their associations, such as ivaa.org.

If you're choosing a new employee for a managerial job that you've been handling yourself, you'll want someone who has the ability to lead people without being a tyrant. If you're delegating a task that involves working with people most of the day, you'll want someone who is not shy but for whom being around people and lots of conversation 40 hours per week is an energy-booster. If you're turning over the tasks of keeping the accounting records, you'll want to find someone who is analytical and not overly creative. Some people work best in a team environment all day, others like to work independently all day, and many prefer a mix of the two. Keep these ideas in mind when matching people to a job.

Arrange interview questions to help you determine how many other qualities the person has, in order to help you make a decision. You can do this whether you're considering an existing employee, a new hire, or outsourcing to relieve yourself of a task. Ask them to tell you about a work situation they've been in before, the problem that arose, and how they solved it. Think of challenges you've encountered at your business as you've performed the particular task. Briefly highlight a challenge to the interviewee and ask them how they would work with it and solve it.

When should you give a task to an employee and when should you outsource it? Outsourcing changes about every decade. New businesses spring up in different parts of North America regularly that no one had previously considered to hire for outsourcing. Years ago, cleaning services were sold by word-of-mouth. Today, many cleaning service businesses are listed in the Yellow Pages. During the 1980s, it was difficult to find someone who could truly help a small business with computer set-up. Today, you can ask two friends and your cousin for referrals and get several computer specialists to choose from who work with small businesses. If you bring your dog to your business place and your dog "does his business" in your yard, you can even hire someone to clean up the dog poop from your yard! Many services are available so that you can get things done for your business without doing those tasks yourself (and before you're ready to hire an employee for the task).

You can outsource your bookkeeping. If you manufacture products, you can outsource the prototype creation to another firm. If your employees need to be trained on computer hardware or software, you can outsource the training. You can pay a freelancer to create a PowerPoint presentation. And if your place of business is outside of your home, *please* bring in someone to clean the bathrooms!

Whether you want to hire an employee to take over certain tasks or outsource the work to a firm is entirely up to you. With an employee, you have to handle the management of the employee in your business, but you have more control. With outsourcing, you'll usually have less management headaches, but occasionally the people are not available when you need them.

Getting back to Kevin's story, in order for his business to increase sales, Kevin knew that he had to hire new salespeople. He wanted two people he could train in his own methods. When I started working with him, each of the new salespeople had been in place for about eight months. One was doing fairly well; the other was not.

I asked Kevin how the other people were doing with the responsibilities he gave them. He responded that the company running his technology was working out well, but that his employee who was handling the customer issues and collections did not seem to have much success.

I sat in on a staff meeting one day in order to make a connection with their business and their personalities. It gave me the information I needed to consult with Kevin more effectively.

A year earlier, Kevin identified responsibilities that he could give to others in order to get the business on a growth pattern, and he identified those tasks well. For some areas, he delegated well and in others he did not.

There are times when simply delegating a responsibility does not work well. Certain areas of a business are not simply skill-driven; they are *personality-driven*. Because of this, a business owner or manager needs to *duplicate* himself or herself in order to grow their business. (Fortunately, this is *not* about cloning yourself!) Rather, this means that they need to find people whose personalities are similar to theirs in order to delegate successfully, especially when they're delegating a task or activity that they previously performed themselves.

As I worked with Kevin, he came to see that when he hired the two salespeople, one had a personality similar to his and one did not. His customers and prospects were used to his outgoing personality and expected his new salespeople (who were "out in front") to be similar. By now his business was growing and he had been thinking of adding another salesperson. We decided that creating a new position for sales strategy would be a better position for the current salesperson who was not doing quite as well. (That guy knew sales technically, but the customers were just expecting him to be a lot like Kevin, which he wasn't.) Next, Kevin set out to find another salesperson with similar qualities to himself in order to *duplicate himself.*

When Kevin realized that he also needed to duplicate his personality with the employee he chose to handle the customer issues and collections, he decided to find someone new to take over those responsibilities. This decision was much to the relief of the employee originally chosen, who had plenty of work just with the accounts receivable. He found someone who wanted to work 20 to 25 hours a week who seemed cut out of the same mold as he, and his customers took to this person immediately.

Kevin learned the difference between *delegation* and *duplication.* Both are important to increasing your profit and decreasing your stress. Each involve giving work to other people, whether to current employees, new employees, or to another business. One of the keys is to delegate the tasks, activities, and responsibilities that are not your strengths and to do that first. Other people have strengths in areas that you do not, and it is important to get those tasks off your plate.

Another key is to identify your responsibilities for which other people, such as your customers, have come to expect *you*, your *personality*, and what you bring to the table. When it is time to find other people to take over some of these duties, identify your strengths, qualities, and characteristics that make you shine. Find people with similar traits in order to successfully duplicate yourself for those responsibilities. This will increase the likelihood that the people you choose will succeed.

Here is a great example of *delegation* vs. *duplication*. People who are devoted fans of the TV show *Desperate Housewives* ever since it first aired loved the first season. They raved about it. In the second season, however, fans claimed the show wasn't as good as in the first season. It wasn't as funny. The stories weren't as engaging. The writing wasn't nearly as good as in the first season. What happened?

The producer of the show, Marc Cherry, wrote the original programs and lead the writing team in season one, doing much of the writing himself. However, producing a 60 minute weekly show involves long hours—12-hour days, five or six days a week. So for the second season, Marc delegated the writing to a new team of highly qualified, talented writers and took himself out of the writing team. However, these new writers didn't write similarly to how Marc writes, so the fans saw a show that didn't keep the same flavor of dark comedy that kept them watching the show in the first season week after week.

What could Marc Cherry have done differently? Rather than merely delegating the writing task to talented writers, he should have *duplicated* himself when selecting the writers by choosing people who thought, dreamt, and wrote like he does. By duplicating himself, he could have ensured that the *"Desperate"* fans loved the second season and remained loyal viewers.

During the third season of *Desperate Housewives*, I read an article in the beginning of that television season stating that Marc Cherry had a new writing team and that he was regularly involved with that team in order to teach them how he thinks and how he writes the show. He took a cautionary approach: choosing new writers who *probably* create and write as he does, but he is spending more time with them to ensure that they catch his thoughts and his mind, thereby *duplicating* himself with his new team.

By "duplication," an owner actually scouts out someone who is similar to himself in various areas so that the customers experience whatever they've come to expect from the owner. Typically, tasks that are delegated in a duplication manner are in sales and customer service. In Marc Cherry's case, the task was *writing* for the audience (and the audience is one of Marc's customers; his other customers are the network and the sponsors). If an owner has been heavily involved in operations, thereby interfacing with many employees (not with traditional customers), turning that task over to someone new who is similar in many ways to the owner is also a smart move. In the case of operations, the "internal customers" are the employees with whom the operations manager works daily.

Where *delegation* involves identifying the right person for a task based on skills, experience, and personality to fit the task, *duplication* involves the same *plus* finding someone similar to the owner (particularly in personality but also in skill set) who can handle the task well and give the people on the "receiving end of the task" a similar feeling and experience as they got from working with the owner when he performed the task.

Whereas delegation is choosing the person for the job based on those three criteria (skills, experience, and personality), duplication is done when an owner recognizes that a group of people, such as customers, want to do business with a certain type of personality that they've become accustomed to (such as the owner), so the owner chooses his replacement for the task with someone who is like a "duplication" of himself. Customers therefore get a similar experience when they work with the new person as they did when working with the owner.

Delegating or duplicating well starts with identifying various tasks you perform for your business and evaluating them as your own strength or weakness. Take some time to identify those areas. Go through the table on the following page; make notes in your journal or wait until you are working in the Application section at the end of the chapter. Add any responsibilities you handle that are not listed on the table.

Business Responsibility	My Strength	My Weakness	Somewhere in Between
	(Place a ✓ in the column that applies)		
Contacting prospects			
Building a relationship with prospects			
Closing the sale			
Ongoing relationships with current customers			
Handling customer issues			
Managing Accounts Receivable			
Collections			
Choosing vendors			
Building relationships with vendors			
Getting good terms with vendors			
Managing Accounts Payable			
Keeping current with cashflow			
Overseeing financial ratios and indicators			
Employee relations			
Training employees well			
Dealing with employee issues			
Keeping technology current in the office			
Operations (when selling a product)			
Developing new products &/or services			
Developing new ways to sell products &/or services			
Creating letters & other items to mail out			
Dealing with paperwork			
Responding to e-mail, mail, and faxes			
Administrative tasks			
Other:			
Other:			
Other:			

Delegation

Delegate the responsibilities you identified in the table above as your weaknesses as soon as possible. Identify other people for whom those areas are strengths. Can you delegate any of these responsibilities to a current employee? If not, are you in a position to hire a new person or to engage an outside service to take over that task?

Look at the "tasks and activities" you noted earlier in the chapter called *"Change Your Way of Doing Business"*. Consider delegating the activities, tasks, and projects that *do not* fall into your top three to five high-yield responsibilities. Make a list of them, and then put the list in the order in which you believe you need to get them off your plate.

Delegation of your responsibilities to employees needs to include training and re-training. See the chapter titled *"Lead Great Teams"* for more information about taking the delegation concept further and to ensure that the delegation of your responsibilities is successful.

Duplication

If you continue to do everything yourself that you identified as a strength, you will either burn out or your business will not grow (or both). Eventually, you will need to hand over some of these responsibilities to an employee, a business partner, or an outside service.

Duplicate yourself in order to grow and to make more room for success. Check the tasks you identified in the previous table as your strengths (also see the "tasks and activities" you noted earlier as your high yield/high return activities in the chapter called *"Change Your Way of Doing Business"*).

You need to identify people *who are like you* to take over some (or all) of those responsibilities.

Have you ever given some of your important tasks to someone who didn't perform those tasks well? Perhaps that person had strengths in other areas, but they did not shine in the areas where you shine.

In order to grow your business and increase profit, you need to find other people to take on some of the work (even though you are great at doing it). You only have so many hours available to you in a day (and the goals we're striving to attain are to increase profit *and* decrease stress).

The mistake many business owners often make is to choose someone for their "strength" responsibilities who is not a good fit. The person chosen is often too different from the owner. When other people, such as your customers, become accustomed to your style, introducing someone new who is quite different from you can create time-consuming problems for you, such as discomforted customers calling to have you solve problems just when you thought you gave the issues to the new employee. (And the idea is to create more time for yourself, not less!) When the responsibilities given to the new person involve relating to people who have become accustomed to dealing with you (prospects, customers, employees, vendors, etc.), it is important that the person you choose is similar to you. The more qualities they have that match yours, the better.

What qualities in you *really shine* when you perform certain responsibilities? Make a list of your responsibilities, and then for each, note the quality about you that really shines when you handle that responsibility for your business. Here is an example. Start a list like this one in your journal:

Responsibility	My Qualities That Shine
Customer relations	Positive; handle problems well
Working with staff	I'm sympathetic

Keep in mind that when you select an employee who is similar to you to take over all or part of a responsibility that you do well, it may create some temporary tension. Prepare yourself ahead of time to deal with conflicts that might arise. The responsibility you hand over may have been "your baby," but every baby must grow up and move on.

Choose someone for your "strength responsibilities" who is teachable and who will commit to the length of time you require; someone who is willing to learn from you, but who may or may not be someone who already has experience in the area. Even though some conflict may eventually arise between you and the person taking over the duty, choose someone whose personality fits well with yours.

As with delegation, duplication needs to include training and retraining. See the chapter titled "*Lead Great Teams*" for more information about taking the duplication concept further and to ensure that handing over your responsibilities is successful.

Automation

Some responsibilities can be automated. For example, following sales made to customers, a system could send out follow-up letters to ask customers about their buying experience, to thank new customers for their business, and/or to inform customers of your other products or services. Someone could be trained to operate the system.

More and more automation is available via the Internet. Many types of communication tools exist, there are Internet companies that provide survey capabilities, and the sky is the limit regarding the future options that will be available to keep you connected with your customers, vendors, and employees.

You—the Delegator!

- Remember that you can delegate to employees, contractors, outside services, or technology/automated services.
- Identifying the tasks, activities, or responsibilities that need to be delegated is the first key.
- Identifying the right people for the tasks, activities, or responsibilities is the second key.
- The third key is training well and retraining later. The time spent *preparing* for training and then *actually training* those to whom you delegate will give you a big payoff down the road.

Sum it Up

I hope you're having some great ideas about delegating tasks, focusing more on your high-yield activities, and putting together a plan to pull it together. Update your journal with your ideas and use the Application section to map out a successful plan.

****

All of the topics you've read about so far involve you, *the entrepreneur*, being a leader. In the next chapter, we dive into how you can become a more effective leader who leads great teams, whether the people you lead are your employees or several outsourced folks who help you run your business.

Application

Let's go back to the table shown in this chapter.

Business Responsibility	My Strength	My Weakness	Somewhere in Between
	(Place a ✓ in the column that applies)		
Contacting prospects			
Building a relationship with prospects			
Closing the sale			
Ongoing relationships with current customers			
Handling customer issues			
Managing Accounts Receivable			
Collections			
Choosing vendors			
Building relationships with vendors			
Getting good terms with vendors			
Managing Accounts Payable			
Keeping current with cashflow			
Overseeing financial ratios and indicators			
Employee relations			
Training employees well			
Dealing with employee issues			
Keeping technology current in the office			
Operations (when selling a product)			
Developing new products &/or services			
Developing new ways to sell products &/or services			
Creating letters & other items to mail out			
Dealing with paperwork			
Responding to e-mail, mail, and faxes			
Administrative tasks			
Other:			
Other:			
Other:			

Place a checkmark in the appropriate column for each row's task.

Afterward, put a *star* to the left of any task that you checked as a *weakness*.

Then *circle* the tasks that you checked as a *strength*.

List the starred weaknesses below:	How can you delegate this task to someone else? How soon can you delegate it? What will it cost to delegate it to someone else?

Now here's a clincher. Are there any tasks you noted as weaknesses (or somewhere in between) that could be high-yield, money-making activities? If so, list them below and start to answer the column on the right:

Task that was noted as a weakness (or in between) that could be high yield:	How might you build this into a strength for yourself? If it would take too long for this to become one of your strengths, how can you best delegate it so that it still makes money for your business?

List all of the circled strengths below:	For each strength, describe whether the task is a high yield activity that is related to bringing money into the business, or whether the task is not high-yield and, even in the long term, does not really bring in money:

Now, go back to the previous table and *circle* any tasks that are strengths for you that do not necessarily bring money into the business.

Then list those tasks in the table below and fill in the right column with answers to the questions in the column header:

Strength task that is not high yield:	How can you delegate this task to someone else? How soon can you delegate it? What will it cost to delegate it to someone else?

Now you're left with your high-yield strengths. Were you able to come up with three, four, or five high-yield tasks that are your strengths?

List your high-yield strength tasks below:	Brainstorm ideas for how you can spend more of your work time on each of these high-yield activities. (This is after you have gained some time in your schedule by delegating the other tasks in the previous tables!)

Sometime, you may find it necessary to even delegate certain activities to people who work similarly to yourself, thereby *duplicating yourself.*

List tasks that you might delegate some day by duplicating yourself:	Why do you think it would be best to duplicate yourself when you give this task to someone else? What characteristics about yourself would be important for someone to have before they take over that task?

Lead Great Teams

"Leadership is the activity of influencing people to cooperate toward some goal which they come to find desirable and which motivates them over the long haul."

—Orway Tead

*L*arry owns a trucking company in the Chicago area. All of his employees are truckers. He does not have any additional office help. He uses his accountant to help him get somewhat organized, but other than that he basically handles all of the daily operations himself.

Larry gets up early every weekday and leaves the house by 5:30 a.m. He thinks he doesn't overwork himself because he is home every day by 4 p.m. (and many days by 3:30 p.m.). However, Larry has not taken an actual vacation in seven years. It also has been three years since he has gone with his wife, Tina, on a weekend away to nearby Wisconsin or Michigan. When Tina brings this up for discussion, Larry tells her that he went with her to Las Vegas two years ago, to which she replies they went to Las Vegas to attend his niece's wedding; otherwise he would not have gone there, either.

Tina knows that she needs occasional vacations, so she schedules time away with friends. At first, Larry didn't seem to care that she was having fun without him, going on ski trips, going to Hawaii, and visiting a friend in San Diego. A couple times recently, though, he seemed a little agitated. Tina reminded him about the fact that she would be happy to go on vacation with him, and that even a weekend away would be great. But Larry just doesn't seem willing or able to pull himself away from the business for long. Even the fact that he is reachable by cell phone at any time doesn't change his outlook about scheduling time away.

Larry is the only person on his company's team (other than the occasional use of his accountant). All of his employees are truck drivers, but not people to whom he can delegate tasks. He makes good money, has a beautiful home, consistently has two luxury cars that he trades often for fun, and has owned a boat or two over the years. He is also stressed out, overweight, and has health issues. He is a man without any real team members, and so he cannot get away from his business mentally or physically.

Are you the type of business owner who, when you leave your business for the day, the weekend, or for a vacation, cannot get the business out of your mind and emotions?

Do you feel that you need to call an employee or business partner regularly to find out what is going on at the company, even while you're at a resort or at your family vacation home? Have you ever heard your children or your spouse *sigh* when you call someone at your business?

In the last chapter, you learned about how delegating tasks significantly frees up your time so that you can focus on the business activities that yield you the most profit for your time. When you delegate, you automatically create *teams* of people within your organization. Likewise, when you put together a team, you create a systemized way of carrying out delegation.

"Leading great teams" means that you actually have people to lead. Once you identify people to whom you will delegate responsibilities, or decide areas in which you will duplicate yourself by finding people similar to yourself, you automatically have a team to lead. The people on your teams are also the people to whom you delegate responsibilities that are not your strengths and to whom you give responsibilities when you duplicate yourself. As you read earlier, this will contribute to decreasing your stress level, making more room for success in your life, and boosting your potential to increase your profit.

Once you delegate tasks to other people (who form into teams), you will meet with them regularly to educate and motivate. They need regular contact with you in order to receive direction so that they can be ready participants in your business. They will look to you to lead their teams. Making a plan to delegate will go a long way to catapulting your business to new levels of success. *Leading great teams* starts with these people. When you have established your teams through delegation, you can apply the team-leading activities in this chapter to those teams in order to create an environment where your team members flourish.

Before we get into more detail about leading great teams, I want to spend a moment telling you about the type of team you *don't* want in your business. Have you ever worked for a company where a team was dysfunctional? A dysfunctional team is a lot like a dysfunctional family. They will zap your energy and suck you dry. They fight and they argue in destructive ways. They cut each other down—including other people's ideas and other people personally. Please get it into your mind that you do not want any of the teams associated with your business to act in dysfunctional ways. Not only are these types of teams bad for you; they are bad for your business.

If you develop your people into *great teams*, however, they will make your life easier as they produce more, get along well with each other, work out conflict in constructive manners, and give you the ability to get away from the office occasionally, as you can trust them to competently handle the business while you're gone.

Leading your business includes leading great teams. When teams become great, they can help to alleviate your stress. In addition to that, great teams give you the ability to increase your profit exponentially.

What types of teams can you design?

Create Three Types of Teams

You can actually create three different types of teams for your business. The first is your business team, which includes mostly in-house people. The second is your advisory team, and that includes various outside people with particular skill-sets or businesses of their own that can help you. The third is your innovation team, which includes friends in business who can help each other with new ideas.

Your Business Team

Your business team consists of your staff and business partners (if you have co-owners). It could also include consultants who regularly perform work for your company. These are people to whom you delegate responsibilities and who you use to duplicate yourself, as discussed in the previous chapter.

Employees and business partners will expect that you all work together as a team. Consultants will be happy that you ask them to be involved in your business team. Let them know how often you will meet and the types of topics that will be discussed. Later in this chapter, you'll read more ideas for how to work with this team (and the others, as well).

If you do not have employees or a business partner right now, you can still create the advisory team and innovation team.

Your Advisory Team

The advisory team consists of various business people who service you in one way or another. It could include people such as:

- a financial advisor;
- your accountant;
- an insurance representative;
- your banker;
- your business coach;
- a website designer and/or graphic designer;
- an advertising expert;
- a public relations person;
- your attorney;
- a technical expert;
- a sales & marketing consultant;
- a recruiter or human resources group (if you have more than a few employees).

These team members are mainly your outside paid consultants. In the previous chapter, you learned that this team can also include people to whom you delegate certain tasks. Anyone to whom you outsource services belongs on this "team." While you will not typically get this entire team together at one time, you may have occasion to have one or two of them at a meeting at the same time, perhaps even along with an employee or two. For example, you might have your outside accountant, a software expert for your financial accounting software package, and an employee who works with that software in a meeting together. Likewise, you might have a marketing specialist in a meeting with your web designer so that you're all "on the same page" regarding how your web site will work well as a marketing tool.

Your Innovation Team

The innovation team is a group of business friends who get together to brainstorm ideas. When you ask for a meeting with them, you request that they get together to brainstorm for you and to give you feedback regarding your ideas. You also offer to do the same for them at a later date. This is something you do for each other regularly (say, monthly or bimonthly) without charging each other. (For instance, you might meet from 11 a.m. to 1 p.m. and the "receiver" for the day provides lunch.)

Apply Your Teams

Start off by sharing your vision for the company with all of your team members—keep them in the communication loop.

Use your teams to plan the rest of your organization. Even if your business is quite small right now, planning out *who does what* (and *when*) will allow your business growth to occur more smoothly when it is ready to happen.

In an earlier chapter, you reviewed your customers' journey and perfect experience. Building and leading great teams always filters down to how people at your business interact with your customers. Now that you also know about business systems, ask yourself these questions: What systems can be put in place to support getting your business closer to delivering that perfect customer experience? What systems can be engineered to elicit a "Wow!" from some customers? And how can you *use your creation of great teams* to carry out well-planned systems for running your business?

Consider the following:

- For your business team, create employee training and retraining programs that focus on step-by-step procedures that heighten the customers' experiences with your business.
- Produce well-written training manuals to accompany the training.
- Take customer surveys regularly to determine how well your company is succeeding at delivering superb customer service and creating super loyal customers.
- Survey your employees regularly to get their thoughts regarding how well they believe the teams are working together.
- If you do not have the time or the staff to develop and deliver a training plan or training materials, or to survey customers, outsource the work to an outside company.

Educate Your Employees: Recruit, Train, & Facilitate

Educating your employees is composed of three separate tasks: recruiting, training, and facilitating.

Recruiting employees involves finding the right people to interview, applying good interviewing skills when meeting them, and then selecting a good person for the job. If you don't get a good selection of people to interview at the beginning, you're not going to get the right person for the job and you'll spend a lot of your valuable time interviewing people and spinning your wheels doing so. There are many ways to find candidates to interview, such as an advertisement in the want ads of a newspaper, using online venues such as Monster.com (where you can [for a fee] list a job opening or pay to scan online resumes that candidates posted), your own word-of-mouth networking, through professional associations that post job openings for their members, and using a professional recruitment agency.

The type of position you're trying to fill will determine which method you use. Years ago I owned a retail store and when I needed a new employee, I placed an ad in the local newspaper, placed a calligraphic-written sign in the entry way, and told all of my friends that I was looking for additional help. When I was in the corporate world, we always used a professional recruiting agency to find good people to interview. That was before the Internet existed and made this information more readily available! The Internet has made it possible to find qualified candidates in many types of skill and experience levels. Monster.com is probably the most popular web site for employers and candidates. Even six-figure executives have sites available online for recruiting at web sites such as Execunet.com and SixFigureJobs.com.

If you equip yourself with good interviewing skills, you will find it fairly easy to select excellent people for your open positions. Read articles about interviewing, select a book from your library on the subject, and even take a class on interviewing skills at a management training company. When I interviewed young accountants for corporate jobs many years ago, I actually found it easier to select a good candidate than I found it several years later when I needed to hire part-time sales clerks for my retail store. I just got really skilled at "reading people," and figuring out who would work out well in the corporate culture and who would be a pain in the neck. Perhaps it was because, at the corporation, I was interviewing people who were younger than I, whereas at the retail store I mostly interviewed people older than I was at the time. It might be easier to read people who are walking a path we once walked, and more challenging (but not impossible) to read people who are ahead of us in life.

Nevertheless, you can get really skillful at finding good candidates and interviewing them to find the right person for a job.

Once you hire people, training them to do the job well is the next step in your quest to educate. Training involves activities that help people become proficient in a skill or behavior. It can take place in a classroom environment with an instructor and several people being trained at one time. Or it can occur when someone who already has the skills teaches someone who is new during on-the-job training.

By taking the time and expense to train employees you will increase the likelihood that they will perform their job correctly, produce a good product or service, make fewer mistakes, make customers happy, make their fellow employees happy, and make you happy. Without adequate training, employees make more mistakes, cost the company money, and frustrate the people they work with regularly.

Training your people should not be a luxury; it should be a necessity. It consists of not only training for new hires, but instituting continual training for your people (including leadership development for yourself and other leaders in your organization).

Facilitating involves you, the business owner, ensuring that your employees' education while in your employment occurs as effortlessly as possible. This may include your personal involvement or you can delegate facilitation to someone else. Whoever handles the facilitation of educating employees must see it through from beginning to end, making it easy for employees to learn whatever they need to learn to do their jobs well.

When you facilitate this process, you assist in the steps the employee takes in order to make progress. Your facilitation ensures that all aspects of the job and the business are covered and that gaping holes don't exist in the employee's knowledge and expertise. If an employee's education in your business is not facilitated, the employee is left to himself to figure things out. This leads to mistakes, less money earned, and/or more expense for the company.

Years ago I worked in post-sales consulting for a software company. Their new employee facilitation was practically nonexistent. I was basically on my own to figure out company policies, the software, and how to apply the software to the customers' businesses with whom I was expected to consult. This situation cost the company money because I wasn't ready to consult with customers about their software purchase very quickly (which was also the case for any new hire). This was because there was no plan to work with me to get me up to speed in order for me to start bringing money into the company in consulting fees. If someone had facilitated the process, I could have learned to know, understand, and apply the software to several business situations in a few weeks rather than in a few months, and the company would have started earning serious cash from my consulting hours about a month after I took the job. The lack-of-facilitation problem was repeated over and over at this company. Once I knew the software like the back of my hand, I recall going to clients' offices where another software consultant with the company had preceded me, and who was a fairly new hire. Clients complained about the previous consultant numerous times and asked for a replacement (myself), and the consultant they complained about was some poor new guy whose training was never facilitated by anyone. Thus, the customers became angry about being billed for someone's time who didn't have the knowledge to help them.

When you've been in the customer role, how many times have you worked with a company's employee who didn't seem to have the knowledge required to do his job properly? And how did you feel about that? Not too happy, right? And in many cases, it cost that company your business.

Employees should not be responsible to oversee their own education. You, as the business owner, are responsible for seeing to it that employees' education in your business is facilitated and carried out timely and smartly.

Educate Employees about the Company in General

One of the basic pieces of information that all employees need to know involves their education on your company policies and regulations. These are the topics that all employees need to be familiar with in order to work at your company. It is mostly information that is considered of a "human resource" nature. When employees are educated on these topics, it makes their transition into the company culture easier.

One of the initial documents you will need to help you educate employees in this area is an employee company manual. This manual will include information about the following:

• **Company policies**	• **Health benefits**	• **Personal days**
• **Timesheets**	• **Vacation & holidays**	• **Other regulations**
• **Medical leave**	• **Annual reviews**	• **Any other insurance**
• **Company hours**	• **LTD benefits**	• **Pay periods**
• **Expense reports**	• **Sick days**	• **Jury duty**
• **Military leave**	• **ADA compliance**	• **Parking**
• **Lunch breaks**	• **Workers'**	
• **Telephone use**	**compensation**	

Educate Employees on their Tools and Products

Are your people using any tools to do their jobs? ("Tools" include items such as mechanical tools, computers, word processing tools, spreadsheet tools, etc.) Do they know how to use the advanced features of those tools? If not, enroll them in a class to learn those features. You bought the features of the tools; it will only serve your business better if your people know how to use the advanced features of their tools and how to apply them to the business.

Employees also may need to be educated regarding the products or services sold by your business. If they are in sales, customer service, operations involving building the product, or consulting with customers, they need to know about the products or services in order to perform their jobs well.

Educate Leaders to Execute Leadership

What leadership skills do you and your other leaders need to cultivate? Consider taking management classes to beef up your expertise. If you have a business coach, talk with him or her to identify the types of skills you might enhance and then work together to gain those leadership skills. Create a leadership development plan for each leader in your company.

Motivate Your People

As you build your business, you have goals and dreams for your company and for your life that you desire to achieve. Once you hire employees, you want these people to help you realize your goals.

Your employees have their own goals, dreams, and ambitions. As their employer, have you come to the place where you know and understand what their goals are, beyond making enough money to pay their bills? You naturally want employees who are honest and who work hard and apply themselves to their work. Truly, if you take interest in what matters to them, make it "your business" to know their goals, and then help them achieve their goals, they will, in turn, return it to you by helping you achieve your goals.

Get to know what motivates your employees. Some may say they are motivated by money. But what is their *drive* to achieve their own goals? Just as a business coach helps entrepreneurs achieve their business goals, and just as a sports coach helps athletes achieve their performance goals, you, as the employer, can help your employees achieve their professional goals and ambitions. It starts with finding out what those ambitions are, and then _building meaning_ around your knowledge.

What is "building meaning"?

Have you ever been in any type of relationship where another person knew something about you that was important to you, the person led you to believe that he or she would do something positive with that knowledge, and then he or she did nothing? That is the _opposite_ of "building meaning". Likewise, have you ever been in any type of relationship where the other person knew of something important to you and then followed-through with positive action? That positive action allowed you to see that he or she really backed you up and supported you. If you have experienced this, what was it like? How did it feel? That person _built meaning_ around their knowledge of something about you.

So _building meaning around your knowledge_ of your employees' ambitions and goals means _taking action_ to help them reach their goals.

It starts with finding out about your employees' ambitions, goals, and dreams. Next, it means letting your employees know that you hear them. And last, it involves doing what you can to help your employees reach their professional goals.

Once your employees see, hear, feel, and know that you are interested in helping them achieve their goals _and_ that you back up your words with actions, they will eagerly help you achieve your goals more willingly and with more motivation than before.

Schedule Meaningful Meetings Regularly

A meeting is the one place where an entire team is together at once. When you lead great teams, you need to spend time with each team corporately, rather than only spending time with people individually. By holding meetings with an entire team you have the opportunity to lead the team cohesively.

Since you may recall bad experiences with business meetings, the very word "meetings" might make your skin crawl. If you have spent any time in the corporate world during your career, then you may have spent a lot of time in meetings. Sometimes you felt the time spent in certain meetings was a waste of time; other times, meetings zipped by, people got the information they needed, and the meetings were over fairly quickly. What was the difference between these two types of meetings?

In the "waste-of-time" meeting, various things happen that lead people to feel as if they are wasting their time. The leader does not have a handle on the focus of the meeting and staying on track. The people attending the meeting are not informed ahead of time about the topics to be covered. One or two people, even though informed, go off on tangents and are not reigned in.

When meetings are a good use of time, however, the leader is focused, he makes certain the attendees are informed about meeting topics in advance, an agenda is provided at the meeting, and topics that can be discussed between two people are tabled for their own conversation at another time.

Where do you keep your schedule? Get it in front of you and plan meetings with your business team regularly. Here are some possible ideas for your meeting schedule:

- Daily: "Meet" with yourself for 10 to 20 minutes to prioritize your "to do" lists.
- Weekly: Meet with your staff for 1 to 2 hours. Update each other regarding what is happening in your respective areas.
- Monthly: Each month (at one of the regularly scheduled weekly meetings), meet for half a day to a full day. Update each other on your respective areas. Set goals. Formulate strategies to meet those goals. Create a 30-day action plan.

If you plan the daily, weekly, and monthly meetings as shown above, your total meeting time will equal 4 percent to 8 percent of working hours. During these meeting times, you are working "on" the business. Actually, 4 percent to 8 percent is not a lot of time, especially if that time is productive and helps the attendees become well-informed and helps them execute their jobs better.

Have an agenda for your meetings in areas such as:
- Finances
- Sales
- Marketing
- Customer Service
- Resources

- Personnel
- Other issues

Define goals for each meeting and stick to the time and topics allotted. Schedule enough time for discussion.

Remember to *not* do all of the talking (or even most of the talking) at staff meetings. As a leader of great teams, you need to listen. A lot.

Influence Your Business Environment

Leaders always have an effect on the people they lead, either positive or negative. If leaders have a great attitude and positive outlook at work, that will beneficially affect their peoples' attitudes and outlooks. If leaders come into the workplace with a sour disposition and a dark cloud over their heads, surely their people will pick up on that also, and soon most people in that environment will feel the dark cloud over their heads as well.

If your goal is to lead great teams of people, you need to know that one of the keys to helping them become great teams lies with how you choose to influence your business environment. Most people are like sponges, and the people you lead will pick up whatever disposition you bring to the workplace. The good news is, you get to *choose* your attitude and disposition before you arrive at work. The bad news is, if something occurred prior to arriving at the office (such as an argument with your spouse or kids), it will take some internal work on your part to change your mood so that it doesn't result in a negative demeanor before you arrive at your business and affect everyone around you.

If you want your teams of people to work together as *great* teams, be aware of your impact on the business' atmosphere. If your teams are going to succeed, they need for you as their leader to influence the environment in a positive, energetic, constructive manner.

In the late 1990s, I was doing consulting work for various companies and there was often consulting work available at a health-care company about seven miles from my home. I was always booked at other companies, however, when work at this health-care company became available. After missing getting work there several times because I was booked, I recall talking with two of my friends who had worked there (one as an employee and one as a consultant). They worked in different areas of the company and did not know each other. Both of them told me that they didn't like the company because the atmosphere was hostile. They said people were mean. It appeared to be systemic. This is not the type of environment you want to create at your business.

In addition to what you've already read about teams, leading great teams is also about carving out an environment where people can *do business well*. Creating an atmosphere *where your people want to be* will make your business a less stressful place to work than most businesses out there today. A *less stressful* business atmosphere creates an environment where people can get things done well, which translates into a more profitable business.

Envision your business as being a place where your employees look forward to going to work every day. Creating a positive environment at your business starts with you—at the top. Just like parents set the tone in their home for their children, you set the tone for the atmosphere at your business for everyone else.

At your place of business, do you greet each other? Do you give messages to one another politely? Do you talk about each other when the "subject" is not present, and if so, in what manner is that person spoken about? When someone is having a bad day, how does that person act and, in return, how do the others respond to him or her? Is drama viewed as a positive or negative thing at your place of business?

Several years ago I worked on a project for a client that had also engaged a well-known consulting firm. One week at a large team meeting, the client sponsor was out of the office and the consulting firm's on-site manager ran the meeting. He became quite melodramatic about "caring about the project both professionally and personally," and he wondered if anyone else cared. He was quite a controlling character, so this just took the cake. After he made his histrionic statement, I realized that it was March and the Academy Awards were just a week away. I almost burst out laughing—was he trying to get an acting award? This person's controlling personality, coupled with occasional dramatic tendencies, made it difficult for the people around him to get work done well. Trusting him was hard for people, and thus, communication was not as good as it could have been. The project suffered because of it.

Some people call this type of person a "drama queen" or "drama king". I think that drama kings and queens can learn to work with others. They need close accountability, however, to put an end to dramatic behavior, which is connected to their need for controlling others and getting their way. People who exhibit this type of behavior are masters at manipulating others, including those to whom they are supposed to be accountable. They will change stories around and embellish the facts in order to make themselves look better. It takes a strong person to hold a drama king or queen accountable and to help them "get with the program" so that the environment at a business is one in which everyone enjoys working.

What goes into making your business environment better and a great place to work every day? How can it start with you, the leader, as you create a great work atmosphere where your teams can thrive?

When people at your business have an issue with someone else, are they encouraged to discuss it and work it out with that person? Or have you made it easier for people to run to you with their people problems? If you set the tone for people to try to work out their problems with each other first, it will make a difference in the interpersonal conflicts that are bound to arise, and it will make a difference in how well teams work together.

Work toward eliminating personal blame at your company and instead blame systems for problems rather than people. Then work together to discover solutions to fix the systems.

Start Leading Great Teams Now

Leading great teams starts with you: the leader. You (and your co-owners, if you have them) are solely responsible to define, create, and lead your teams, and to fashion the positive atmosphere your teams need in order to help you increase your business profit and decrease your personal stress.

Sum it Up

Where is your business "at" right now in terms of growth? What types of people should be on each of your teams? Do you have enough employees to form a business team? If so, how will you train them on your business systems? Who should belong to your Advisory Team and your Innovation Team? Enter notes to your journal and use the Application section to brainstorm your ideas and to get those ideas to come together so that you're really leading great teams.

★★★★★★★★★★★★★★★★★★★★★★★★

Sales is the lifeblood of a business and marketing is the funnel through which all eventual sales first go. A business without sales cannot exist. In the next chapter, you'll learn some tips about building up your marketing strategies and sales skills.

Application

Your Business Team

Do you currently have business partners or employees? If so, they are on your *Business Team*.

List their names below and write what their role is in the business:

- How often do you want your Business Team to meet?

Your Advisory Team

Have you ever thought about having an *Advisory Team*? Perhaps as you read through the chapter, you realized that you're already working with people as outsourced services who are filling roles that make up some type of Advisory Team (even if that "team" is virtual). Look at the list below and write in the names of people who are currently filling that role:
- Financial advisor:

- Accountant:

- Insurance representative:

- Banker:

- Business coach:

- Web site designer / Graphic designer:

- Advertising expert:

- Public relations specialist:

- Attorney:

- Technical expert (PCs, software, etc.):

- Sales & marketing consultant:

- Recruiter or HR specialist:

For each of the names above, write next to their name how much you pay them for their services. Then consider: Do you feel you are receiving value for your money? If so, why? If not, why not? (and how can you change that?).

For any of the roles above that don't have a person you're working with yet in that capacity, either write in a date by which you might like to have someone chosen for that role or write *"N/A"* if you believe you will not need to have that role filled in the next few years.

Have you ever considered holding a meeting with one or more of your Advisory Team members at one time? As mentioned in the chapter, you could have your accountant and a technical expert who can help you with accounting software at the same meeting. You might have a marketing specialist and your web designer at the same meeting. You might also have your business coach at a meeting (or on a conference call) with your web designer or the marketing specialist or the accountant.

7.1 What ideas are you getting for utilizing the skills of your Advisory Team to the max?

7.2 What combinations of people do you want to get together at one time so that their teamwork comes together to offer you the best possible ideas?

7.3 How often do you want each "combination" to meet?

7.4 What incentive will you give them to meet in this capacity? (For example, do you need to pay them an hourly rate? Do you just need to buy them lunch?)

Your Innovation Team

You read that your Innovation Team consists of a group of business friends and acquaintances who meet together to brainstorm ideas. Each time you meet, your focus is on one team member and their business. The person receiving the help buys lunch or dinner.

The true purpose of this team is innovation and problem-solving. Some people are good at that and some are not. For this team, you may need to stick to people who are either business owners themselves or who at least have an entrepreneurial mindset.

7.5 Who would be great for you to have as members of your Innovation Team?

7.6 How could you approach each person to ask them if they'd be willing to do this? (A phone call? An e-mail?)

7.7 However you approach them, what are you going to say (or write)?

7.8 How often will you propose that you all get together?

7.9 Would meeting from 11 a.m. to 1 p.m. work for you?

7.10 Where would be some good places to meet where you could have a place to talk where you wouldn't be rushed or interrupted, have room to take notes, have a white board or flip chart (if possible), eat a meal, and not be overburdened with scheduling and food and planning?

7.11 How soon can you implement your Innovation Team?

7.12 What do you hope to accomplish with the help of an Innovation Team?

Apply Your Teams

7.13 How can you best communicate your vision for your company with all of your team members?

7.14 How can you use your teams to plan out *"who does what"* in your business?

7.15 How can you use the knowledge and expertise of your team members to get systems in place that deliver to your customers a great customer experience?

Educate Your Employees: Recruit, Train, & Facilitate

7.16 How are you going to find the best employees possible?

7.17 How are you going to increase your interviewing skills?

7.18 So far, how have you trained employees at your company?

7.19 How well has that worked?

7.20 How often do employees make mistakes?

7.21 How often can you get away from the business and trust that the employees can run the business in your absence effectively?

7.22 In what areas can you create (or can someone else on your behalf create) training manuals that teach employees how to run that area of the business?

7.23 How can you successfully use a training manual and on-the-job training to teach a new employee how to do their job?

7.24 Review your company policy manual and ensure that the following topics are covered adequately:

- **Company policies**
- **Timesheets**
- **Medical leave**
- **Company hours**
- **Expense reports**
- **Military leave**
- **Lunch breaks**
- **Telephone use**

- **Health benefits**
- **Vacation & holidays**
- **Annual reviews**
- **LTD benefits**
- **Sick days**
- **ADA compliance**
- **Workers' compensation**

- **Personal days**
- **Other regulations**
- **Any other insurance**
- **Pay periods**
- **Jury duty**
- **Parking**

7.25 What leadership skills do you and your other leaders need to cultivate?

7.26 How can you receive leadership development training?

Motivate Your People

7.27 What are you currently doing to know your employees' ambitions and goals?

If your organization has several layers of people, you can do this goal acknowledgement for one or two layers of employees who report to you, and then teach those people to do the same for their employees.

7.28 Write down at least 10 employees' names below. Across from each, write down their goals, as far as you know them. (These can be goals about their home, money, kids [i.e. college education, etc.], retirement, serious hobbies [i.e. Are any of them weekend race car drivers? Do any desire to write a novel? Are any part of a nonprofit organization that they want to grow?], elderly parents, etc.)

7.29 For any of these people, do you need to find out more about them? If so, *how* and *when* can you do it?

Team Meetings

What do you think about scheduling regular staff meetings?

7.30 What do you like about it?

7.31 What do you not like about it?

7.32 When you compare your likes and dislikes about regularly scheduled meetings, what patterns emerge?

7.33 When you consider that, out of all of your working hours each year, 4 percent to 8 percent of that time will be spent in meetings with your staff, does that sound like a lot of time or not too much time?

7.34 How can you make certain that time spent at staff meetings stays under control, while you and your staff accomplish a lot and communicate well?

Your Business Atmosphere

What is your business environment like right now? (Be painfully honest as you answer this question.)

7.35 What is pleasant about it?

7.36 Do the things you just wrote make everyone look forward to coming there every day?

7.37 What is unpleasant about it?

7.38 If you were not the owner, would you want to come there every day? Why or why not?

7.39 How do you and your employees speak to one another?

7.40 Brainstorm some ideas to create a work environment to which your people look forward every work day when they get up in the morning.

A Few More Things to Consider

7.41 What areas of your business seem to be on your mind a lot?

7.42 In what ways would it be great to not be as concerned about those areas any longer?

7.43 What do you think you can do to change it? Brainstorm some ideas below:

(It is by figuring out ways to solve business problems that you develop systems for running your business better.)

Build Up Your Marketing Strategies and Sales Skills

"Pretend that every single person you meet has a sign around his or her neck that says, 'Make me feel important.' Not only will you succeed in sales; you will succeed in life."

—Mary Kay Ash

*D*an runs a distribution company that he started more than 10 years ago. He is based in Kansas City and has four distribution centers in the U.S. He started the business with two centers and added the other two more recently. When he expanded, he felt the business was ready and could handle the growth, based on the forecast he created earlier with his staff to secure funding to add the new centers.

As I listened to him talk about the business, I realized he was second-guessing his expansion decisions. As I coached him through his apprehension, I found that the sales figures were less than he expected. It appeared that his predictions about sales and marketing in the new regions were not accurate. He needed to revisit sales and marketing strategies for those areas and bring the sales representatives, sales director, and marketing director into discussions about the revisions.

While sales and marketing are two separate activities, we often think of them as going together. *Sales* involves interacting with prospects and customers directly. Activities such as making sales calls and follow-up calls, creating proposals, constructing price quotes, and taking and processing orders are part of the sales process. *Marketing* involves behind the scenes activities that support the sales staff. This can include market research and analysis, competitive analysis, profitability analysis, pricing strategies, and promotional programs. While sales bring revenue to the business, marketing brings sales to the business.

Marketing

Marketing activities *support* the sales processes for your company. Depending on the business you are in, the size of your company, and your location, some marketing strategies will work better for you than others. While this book is not intended to offer a comprehensive look at marketing, it will hopefully get you started in the right (or a new) direction, building marketing strategies that work for your company.

Marketing activities basically create and communicate a message about your products or services. If whatever you do to market your product doesn't come across clearly to prospects and customers, then your marketing activity (or activities) are not working properly. If you fail at marketing, your prospects and customers will not clearly understand what they "get" as a benefit when they buy from you and, therefore, may not buy as much product as they could, may not buy as often as they should, or may not buy at all.

The businesses behind all products and services in the market today have a certain type of customer in mind who will purchase their product or service. For example, a particular software product is intended to be purchased by a certain size company in certain types of businesses (say, companies that manufacture and distribute clothing, and that have $10 million in sales per year will use that particular software product). Even an air freshener product's creators will have a certain customer in mind, and it is not "everyone." For example, air freshener Renuzit's marketing people have intended for their product to be purchased by women who have children still living at home. The intended customer for a product is called the *target market*.

Most products and services have competitors on the market who want to sell to the same customer you want to sell to. It's important to have a good handle on who the competitors are, what they are doing with their products or services, and how they are reaching your target market.

One of the best things you can do to market your business is to develop relationships that create *referral business*. This is extremely cost-effective. It just takes some time on your part to figure out where you will most likely meet people from whom you can receive referral business (and to whom you can *give* referral business), how to create the time to be with these people, and then start referring business to them. It's a mostly unspoken "rule" in business that if you refer business to people, they should also refer business to you.

Many other marketing strategies exist for building awareness of your product with your target market audience. In the pages that follow you'll see a list to choose from. In the early days of building your business, it's wise to be creative and to not overspend on your marketing budget. With time, you'll be able to put more funding into marketing projects.

Speaking of marketing costs, developing a 12-month marketing plan and budget will help you think about the big picture for your marketing efforts, the details that go into fulfilling your marketing plan, and the budget to carry it out.

Once you start implementing your marketing plan, evaluate it regularly to determine if adjustments are required.

Determine Your Target Market

If you haven't done so yet, you need to figure out which people or businesses are in your target market. In fact, even if you've already done that, it's a good idea to evaluate if you're missing anyone who should be in your target market group. Is your product or service sold to a person (i.e. consumers) or a business? (Or is your product a consumer product that you sell to retail establishments? In that case, you have two target markets: the consumer and the retailer.) Once you have a basic idea of who your target market people are, you need to evaluate them. If your target market includes consumers, think in terms of age, gender, socio-economic status, geographic region, etc. If your target market includes businesses, think in terms of business type, size, what they sell, geographic region, etc.

If you are at the point in your business when you are ready to take your products to a new market (such as a foreign country), make sure you know what you're doing!

When the Gerber baby food company decided to expand into Africa many years ago, they ran into big problems, as their product was not selling at all. Upon further investigation into the culture and learning about how food is usually packaged, labeled, and sold in certain African nations, the problem came to light. In many of the countries where they were trying to sell baby food, Gerber found out that food products in those countries (where several languages may be spoken and/or there is high illiteracy) were labeled with pictures depicting what the food product is made of. Shoppers in Africa were horrified when they saw the picture of the baby on the Gerber jar. (*"There is a baby in there?"*)

One of the most popular vehicles that Chevrolet ever produced, the Nova, was a complete flop in Mexico. Even though "Nova" means "exploding star" in English, a Spanish translation can be easily taken as "No Va," which means "Doesn't go." Who would want a car named *"Doesn't Go?"*

If you are planning to move into a new market, do your homework on your new target market. Enlist the assistance of a marketing-related consultant from the foreign country who will ensure that the marketing communications about your product will strike a positive chord with your target market customer.

Sometimes entrepreneurs make the mistake of thinking that just because they've worked very hard on their product and think it's the best, everyone else will think so, too. The business is their "baby," and just like parents think their baby is the cutest and smartest in the world, business owners can mistakenly believe the same because they "know" their product is superior…everyone else will be automatically convinced the product is superior as well. But that isn't necessarily true. Target market customers need a lot more convincing, and the right marketing messages and marketing strategy will help to convince your target market that your product is superior, too. Use marketing strategies to build the belief about the superiority of your product in the minds of your target market.

What are Your Competitors Doing?

Study your competitors. Check out what they are selling and how they are selling it. Find out their marketing strategies. Look into how they run their businesses. Do they have a lot of employees? Or do they use a combination of employees and outside services?

Business owners often make the mistake of not finding out what their competitors are doing (or they *assume* they know everything their competitors are doing). It is also easy to assume you know all about their products and how they market their products. Take the time to really find out. Review their printed materials and their web site. Find out how they make customers happy.

Develop Relationships that Create Referral Systems

Marketing through the people you know already and planning a grassroots marketing effort are cost effective strategies. This includes cultivating existing and new relationships that create referrals.

My grandfather was a master at this. His parents came to the U.S. in the late 1800s, settled in Michigan, and my grandfather left home when he was 18. (You could say they were *not* well-off.) He joined the army, and later got a degree in accounting and started his own accounting firm in Chicago. By the late 1950s/early 1960s, he was a millionaire. Now, how did an accountant get to be a millionaire? He networked well, referred business to other people, people referred business to him, and he invested well. He knew a lot of people in the Chicago area. They all referred business to each other. He served on boards of nonprofit organizations, took people out for lunch and dinner, joined a country club, and golfed. Hey, it wasn't all work—I think he had a lot of fun building business relationships.

For many entrepreneurs, having other people refer prospects to you is a great way to ensure increased sales. In order to develop a referral pipeline, you need to first determine which methods will work best for your business to generate referrals. How can you keep your name and a memory of what you do in front of potential referral sources?

- Create a newsletter (send it by mail or e-mail, either quarterly or monthly). Give value to your readers in the form of information they can use.
- Attend events where the people you want to meet network with each other.
- Speak to groups (plus, gather sign-ups for your newsletter at the speaking engagements).
- Form strategic alliances with different businesses that serve the same types of customers.
- Serve on a nonprofit board or a community committee, on which you will be likely to meet people and develop relationships with those who will refer business to you.

Figure out what works best for you—for your type of business, the stage your business is at currently (i.e. first year, tenth year, etc.), and the amount of time you have available. And remember what you read in an earlier chapter about your high-yield activities (this is one of them).

Consider a Variety of Marketing Strategies

The following is a list of marketing strategies that, while not exhaustive, gives you a good idea of the many options available to you. Consider your sales goals. Think about what marketing methods might work well for your business.

- *Trade shows* – Which trade shows do your prospects attend? Should you get a booth? Should you be a workshop speaker? Should you simply attend to network?
- *Brochures and other printed materials* – What type would work best to reach your prospects in your industry?
- *Web site* – Should you have a simple web site that is an "online brochure", or should your web site be more complex (for example, a web site from which customers can order products directly)?
- *Direct-mail campaigns* – This works well for businesses in certain industries. What has worked well for your competition?
- *Telemarketing* – As for direct mail campaigns, some businesses do well with telemarketing. Do your competitors use this method?
- *Speaking for groups* – Could you reach more prospects by speaking for groups?
- *Print advertising* – Consider advertising in trade magazines, newsletters, and journals.
- *Billboard advertising* – This works well for some businesses; check pricing in your target area.
- *Radio or TV advertising* – This is pricey. Consider advertising on cable TV.

- *Market research* ⎤ It may benefit some businesses to include
- *Competitive analysis* ⎦ analysis results in their marketing materials.
- *Pricing strategies* – Examples of pricing strategies include quantity discounts, seasonal sales, increasing the price of popular products, and lower pricing to sign on new customers.

As you experiment with marketing strategies, make certain to ask new customers how they found out about your business. Keep track of what they say. Some entrepreneurs never ask new customers this question, so they never know how effective their marketing strategies are and which are working best. If you find that 90 percent of your new customers come from referrals from previous customers, invest more in your existing customers and less in other strategies that give you no business.

If you place ads, you can include a phrase that says, for example, "10 percent off your next purchase if you bring in this ad and present it at time of purchase" (and include an expiration date). Or, if your customers order online, it could read, "Order online by 9/30/xx and receive 10 percent off your entire purchase by entering coupon code 'abc 123' before completing your order." By using either of these examples, you will know which ads are having a positive effect. This analysis tells you which marketing activities to keep and increase, which to decrease, and which to stop.

Create a Marketing Plan/Budget

Once you create a marketing plan and budget, keep yourself from making marketing decisions based on impulse. Don't be like the business owner who saw a funny TV commercial on a local cable channel, thought how fun it would be to create his own commercial, did not consider the cost, and went with his impulse. While he had fun making his commercial, the cost sunk his budget for the year. He should have focused on less costly marketing activities and stuck to his plan rather than getting drawn into some other business' funny commercial.

Evaluate Your Plan Regularly

Marketing plans are as good as the paper they're written on. You need to implement the plan and then assess it regularly as to whether certain marketing activities are working or not (and if not, why not?).

Marketing's main objective is to drive people to buy. Marketing activities exist to serve the business by creating more and more sales opportunities. Whether your business actually has sales people on staff or not, sales activities result from good marketing.

Sales

The simple way to break down the sales process is in four steps:

- Find a prospect who is interested in what you are selling because they have a need that your product or service will fill.
- Provide the prospect with the information he or she needs to make a decision to buy.
- Close the sale.
- Follow-up with the customer regarding their level of satisfaction.

Maybe that is a little too simple. Usually several conversations take place between you and your prospect. You often need to know a lot more information about your prospect and their situation in order to position your product or service. Let's review some strategies to build up the sales skills of people at your company. You can use these strategies either for yourself or for your sales staff (if you have them). Choose to implement whatever works for your industry.

Ask Effective Questions

What is your prospect's current situation? If you do not know, ask them.

"What is your situation now?"
"How is that product/service working out for you?"
"What issues are you having?"
"How is that (issue) keeping you from doing
_____ (*fill in the blank*)?"

Ask questions that lead to your benefits.
"What is the ideal solution you're looking for?"
"If you woke up tomorrow and _____ was exactly as you want it to be, what would it be like?"
"What are your goals for _____?"
"Before I go on, if I could make one wish come true for you, what would it be?"

Ask questions to find out what is keeping them from buying.
"Is there something keeping you from making adecision?"
"Are there any issues holding you back?"

Ask about the outcome of their purchase.
"If this works, what difference would it make to your business?"

Offer a Solution

Use a set of statements to respond specifically to the prospect's reply. For example:

Capability: "Having listened to you, I think we can help you."

Fact: "We can provide a specific solution..."

Bridge: "...which means that..."

Benefit: "...we will eliminate the problem..."
or, "...we will provide a solution..."

Outcome: "...so that you will be able to_____."

Evidence: "This has been used by many of our customers, and has worked well."

Trial Close: "How does that sound?"

Here is an example of these statements working together (with the statements shown above <u>underlined</u>):

"<u>Jim, having just listened to you, I think we can help you. We can provide a specific</u> Internet <u>solution</u> that addresses your vendor issues where you have vendors constantly calling your accounts payable group to find out the status of their invoices. <u>That means we will eliminate this problem</u> of constant phone call interruptions and full voicemail boxes for your A/P group <u>so that they can get their work done</u>. Your vendors will be able to go online to check the status of their invoices, including the status of invoice approval, who is holding up the approval process, if A/P has received their invoice, and the expected date of payment. <u>All of our customers love this new technology</u> that they're using with their vendors, and their vendors like it, too, because they can get quick answers to their questions without waiting for a return phone call. <u>How does this sound?</u>"

Resolve Concerns and Objections

If they seem hesitant to purchase, ask about it.

Cushion: "I can appreciate your concerns. Anyone with that concern would feel that way."

Reflect and Clarify: "As I understand it, you can see the value of what I'm proposing, but you're concerned about _____."

Identify any hidden objections: "Is there anything else?"

Respond: (Respond with a solution, evidence, value, explanation, or by educating them.)

Trial Close: "So, can we get started?" or, "So, can we place an order?"

Gain Commitment

Choose a method that works for you and your business to gain commitment from the prospect.

Direct: "Is there any reason why we can't get started?" or, "Is there anything preventing you from trying this?"

Alternative choice: "Would you prefer product x or product y?"

Minor point: "May I assume you would prefer the abc version?"

Next step: "Can we book the first appointment now?"
or, "Can we fill out an order form now?"

Opportunity: "If we start now, we can meet the deadline."

Weighing: "Let's look at the pluses and minuses on a sheet and weigh things out."

Appeal: Simply ask the customer for the sale. This is often used for subsidiary sales after a bigger sale closed.

Compel: "This is the last of its kind in stock."
or, "This is the last day at this price."

Negotiation: Use this method after you know your prospect's main objection and have created a response to it. Repeat his or her objection and then respond to it. "You mentioned that the product you need is either 15 feet or 20 feet long. If I can get you one that's 15 feet, will you buy it?"

Provisional: Use this method after you know your prospect's main objection and have created a response to it. As you're talking, ask him or her to make a provisional commitment. "Would you buy this product if I could find one that's 15 feet?"
You want them to respond affirmatively to this question. For example, you want them to say, "I'll buy one that's 15 feet if you have it." You get the customer to take the initiative by stating his or her demand, you meet the demand, and you easily make the sale.

Put on a Show

Does anyone at your company do sales presentations? If so, make sure they put on a show! There is nothing worse for a sales presentation than a boring speaker who cannot connect with the audience. Products may malfunction, computers might not work properly, but a presenter who handles those problems well will not lose the audience. Your listeners will forgive you for certain blunders, but not for boredom.

In order to put on a show for your prospects:
- Speak clearly and pronounce words correctly.
- Learn to *not* speak in a monotone; add vocal variety to your speech.
- Speak more slowly when you talk about important points.
- Speak faster at minor points.
- Speak more loudly and boldly at your strong, main points.
- To draw your prospect in when you tell them something that could be construed as confidential, speak in a lower, slightly quieter voice.
- Appeal to your prospects' sense of sight and hearing.

If your product has a smell, taste, or touch, use those senses, too.
- Demonstrate the product: Turn gadgets on and off.
- If possible, use your prospect in part of your demonstration.

By all means, do not annoy your audience. One of my former clients, Cathy, was an executive at a soda pop bottling company. She told me that during a software demonstration, she asked the salesman to show the product doing something in particular. He responded, "Sure, babe, whatever floats your boat!" Cathy was the main decision-maker for that purchase. I'm sure you can guess, as good as that software product might have been, the company did not purchase it. That salesman lost the sale.

Sum it Up

You may have read this chapter straight through, without taking any notes or jotting down any thoughts. That's okay. When you get a chance, read through it again. This time, take notes in your journal and use the Application section. Which marketing strategies stand out to you as possibilities for your company over the next 12 months? Which sales skills do you want to practice and build up to ensure you do not lose a sale?

★★★★★★★★★★★★★★★★★★★★★★★★

Whether you've already started making a lot of money or if you're on the brink of catapulting your business to new levels of profit, you need to know how to interpret the financial health of your business. The next chapter takes you through the basics that all entrepreneurs should know about handling their finances. It will help you determine your financial goals and when you know you've reached them.

Application

Marketing

8.1 Define your target market:

8.2 What are your competitors doing to sell more products/services?

8.3 How can you develop more relationships that lead to referral systems for your business?

8.4 Which marketing methods has your company utilized?

• How have these methods served you well?

• How have these methods not served you well?

8.5 Which of the marketing strategies listed in the chapter piqued your interest? Write them below.

• For each strategy above that would cost a significant amount of money, put a dollar sign $ next to it.

• For each strategy that would be cost effective, put an asterisk * next to it.

8.6 Which of the marketing strategies you wrote are good possibilities for the coming year? *Highlight* those.

8.7 Which of the marketing strategies are good possibilities for two years from now? *Circle* those.

Start to develop a plan to implement the highlighted and circled marketing strategies. As you come up with definite ideas and tasks you need to accomplish or delegate, schedule them into your calendar.

Also schedule a review periodically to evaluate how your current marketing plan is coming along.

Sales

8.8 What does your *sales organization* look like today?

8.9 What do you want it to look like five years from now?

8.10 What sales strategies has your company practiced thus far?

• How has it worked well?

• How has it not worked well?

Do you want to develop a new sales plan?

8.11 What sales ideas crossed your mind as you read this chapter? Brainstorm ideas without critiquing.

8.12 Now go back to your ideas above and write down *what is possible* for each.

Go back and review the "*Ask Effective Questions*", "*Offer a Solution*", "*Resolve Concerns and Objections*", and "*Gain Commitment*" sections. How can these suggestions help you and your sales staff make more (and better) sales?

Handle Your Finances
with Finesse

*"It sounds extraordinary, but it's a fact that
balance sheets can make fascinating reading."*

—Mary Archer

*J*im is a "solopreneur" and consultant who works on a variety
of technical projects for several clients. Most of the time he
works at his client's site, as he needs to be close to their
hardware and technical employees. He handles his own
accounting duties using a small business software package.
Since he enjoys making money, he has no problem creating
timely invoices for clients. He generates invoices according to
his contract terms and delivers them promptly. His business
does not have many expenses. Writing himself a payroll
check is high on his list of priorities, and payroll is the business'
largest annual expense. He gets very busy, though, so other
accounting duties take a back seat.

For Jim, his biggest issue became paying his payroll
withholding taxes on time. At his business' payroll level, he
was required to pay his federal withholding taxes monthly
and his state withholding taxes quarterly. Even though he can
easily pay these taxes online, being a busy man, forgetfulness
about payroll taxes settled in. Not only did he forget to pay
the taxes on time, he also forgot how much of his bank balance

was a payable to either the federal or state governments for the payroll taxes.

The government does not take kindly to not being paid on time. I once read an article in which the author wrote, "You do not want to get to know an I.R.S. agent on a first-name basis!"

So what is Jim to do? He is a busy man. He feels he does not have time for the financial activities he considers "extra", including the mess he got himself in by paying his payroll withholding taxes late.

Consider another business owner, Kathy. She owns a home furnishings retail store in a metropolitan area. She has two full-time and eight part-time employees, beautiful inventory, and built good relationships with her suppliers and key customers in her area. Unlike Jim, Kathy uses the services of her accountant's office to handle paying her business' payroll taxes timely on her behalf, and the accountant's staff oversees bills paid by Kathy's clerical employee to ensure all payments are for legitimate expenses.

Since the accounting firm does such a good job at handling the financial details (and Kathy doesn't enjoy doing that part of the business anyway), she hasn't educated herself on basic financial information for small businesses that could help her run her business better, smarter, and more profitably. To her, the financial data seems boring. After looking at it for one minute, she feels like she needs a nap.

Even though Kathy is having a great time owning her business, she is "in the dark" regarding financial details that could help her make more profitable decisions for her business and her future.

Whenever I talk to people like Jim who own a very small business, I tell them that they either have to take care of all of their financial business themselves, or they need to find people who will do it (or part of it) for them. For entrepreneurs like Kathy, I let them know that familiarizing themselves about basic small business financial information can lead to making more money. The key is, as a business owner, one way or another you must *take control of your finances*.

Consider this formula:

Financial control = Less stress = Peace of Mind

If you want less stress in your life, you need to get control of your finances and handle them with finesse.

What are the "Financials" You Should Review?

Your accountant (and/or your accounting software system) provides you with two basic financial statements: the Profit & Loss Statement (also known as the "P&L Statement" or "Income Statement") and the Balance Sheet. You may also review a third called the Cashflow Statement.

- Profit & Loss Statement: All of your business' sales revenues and expenses appear on the profit & loss statement. Subtracting the total expenses from the total revenues shows whether your business has a net profit or net loss. This statement covers a specific period of time, such as a year, a quarter, or a month.
- Balance Sheet: Any business accounts that are not revenue or expense appear on the balance sheet, namely assets, liabilities, and equity. The total of the

business' assets equals the total of the liabilities plus the equity (and the equity includes the net profit or net loss of the business from the P&L statement). The balance sheet is actually a financial "picture" of your business taken on one particular day.

• Cashflow Statement: This statement shows the cash coming in to the business (from customers paying their bills) and the cash going out of the business (from the business purchasing products and services) for a certain time period. The statement can show one month's, quarter's, or year's data. Or you can create a spreadsheet that shows several time periods in columns across the report.

As part of your financial overview, you should also look at *financial ratios* (also known as *financial metrics*). The numbers for these ratios come from either the Profit & Loss statement or the Balance Sheet. Each ratio tells you something about your business' financial status. Common ratios are defined and described in this chapter.

By learning a few basic methods for reviewing financial statements and ratios, you get a better handle on the financial health of your business. If you focus on getting comfortable reading and interpreting your own financial data, you will increase your likelihood to make better financial decisions for your business. Just like a new driver needs to learn how to read a roadmap and his car's gauges for a trip (helping him decide how he will journey from his starting point to his destination, along with stops, exits, and forks in the road—plus warning signs from the car's gauges), so you need to accurately interpret your financial data in order to notice trends in spending, acknowledge warning signs that require adjustments, and make timely decisions that make or save the business money.

Business owners who ignore reviewing their financial data place themselves at risk of ignorance of their financial situation. Being ignorant of their financial situation can lead to making poor decisions regarding money (such as spending too much on certain areas of the business), making money-related decisions too late, and not seeing warning signs soon enough (and getting themselves in a financial hole that is difficult to dig out of).

By practicing good financial management, you can improve your business' bottom line, which means more money for your business to grow and more money in your pocket.

What are the consequences to you, as the business owner, of leaving *financial data review* to other people (or ignoring it altogether)?

- Entrepreneurs who ignore reviewing their financial data place themselves at risk of going into a downward financial spiral and not finding out before it's too late. That ignorance can have a "ripple effect" on their business.
  - For example, that lack of knowledge could lead them to spend more than they should. By spending too much money rather than waiting until their cashflow improves, they risk emptying their cash account when other more important bills are due. When cash suddenly runs low, some bills won't be paid on time or an owner could be late to make payroll.

- If customers are paying bills late, an owner who doesn't review his financials won't necessarily know and will not initiate action to receive payments more timely. This will keep the business from getting cash on a timely basis. (This is also known as "slow receivables") Slow receivables lead to not being able to pay your own bills on time.
- If he is spending too much in certain areas, the financials would tell him that, but without reviewing the statements, he won't know. Without knowing this information, an owner will not make adjustments to his spending, and he'll continue spending too much money in the same areas over and over.
- Without reviewing a few simple financial ratios, an owner won't know, for example, his ability to meet his current obligations (i.e. "current bills").

It's enough to make you want to get a basic education in financial data, isn't it?

Take Your Financial Prowess to a New Level

Entrepreneurs whose businesses are larger than "solopreneur" status or micro-businesses have already tackled Jim's problem. By now, those of you with "larger" small businesses have an outside accountant who handles a variety of financial work for you. What they do for you depends on the type of business you own and the sheer quantity of invoices sent, bills received, checks deposited, and checks paid. You may have employees who handle some financial duties for you, either on a clerical level or a controller level.

Perhaps your business is a micro-business, but you foresee growth in the near future. Getting ready for growth now and planning to handle the financial responsibilities that go along with it is a great idea. It will create more room for that growth in your business, without overwhelming you.

To handle your finances well, your focus at this point should be on several areas, such as:

- Forecasts (also known as "Budgets")
- Financial statements
- Pricing
- Debt reduction
- Controlling costs
- Reserves

Some of your financial responsibilities regard the *past*, some deal with the *present*, and others help you focus on the *future*.

Review the Financial Past

Examining your financial results helps you understand more about where you need to go. It starts with reviewing your financial statements and then analyzing ratios (also known as *financial metrics*).

If you are doing this analysis yourself rather than having an accountant do it for you, remember that the payoff for this extra work comes later. By getting a clear financial picture, you will be able to make better business decisions that eventually lead to making more money.

Why should you review your financial history, and what does it do for you?

Look at the financial statements and metrics in order to know how much money was made and spent; which areas of the business spent the most money; which products or services made the most money; your styles, patterns, and tendencies for spending; how quickly customers pay their invoices; how quickly you pay vendor invoices; if you will run out of cash in two weeks; if certain expenses are unusually high, and which areas of the business are most profitable.

Some business owners prefer to not review their financial statements or metrics. Because they don't perform a regular review, they actually look at their financial picture as if it's out of focus (though they may be unaware of it). Because of this, they don't truly know how they're doing in any of the areas just mentioned in the previous paragraph. However, by reading the financial statements and reviewing ratios regularly, business owners get a clear picture of their financial situation.

There really are some great benefits to reviewing your financial data. By getting a clear picture of your financial situation via reading the data regularly, you will notice trends in spending, interpret warning signs accurately (that allow you to make timely adjustments), and you will be led to make financial decisions that improve the bottom line of your company.

Start by reviewing your monthly financial statements. As mentioned earlier, this includes your Profit & Loss statement (P&L, aka "Income Statement") and Balance Sheet, at minimum, and perhaps a Cashflow statement. All of these statements need to be prepared regularly and timely.

Most small business accounting software packages will create the P&L statement and Balance Sheet (with a comparison to the previous year's results at the same time of the year, if you wish). Also, a query can be written for other more advanced software packages to create the comparisons that you require. In addition, a few accounting software packages will calculate the percentage change for each line item or subtotal, if you choose to compare the current period's results with a prior period. If that is not possible, have someone load the numbers into a spreadsheet software program, such as Microsoft Excel, to perform the calculations. If you have an outside accountant, he or she will create these statements for you annually, and also quarterly or monthly, depending on the size of your business.

It's a good idea to decide ahead of time which expenses your business will incur over a year. Typical business expenses fall into these categories:

- inventory
- payroll
- advertising
- supplies
- repairs & maintenance
- travel
- meals & entertainment
- postage
- dues & subscriptions
- professional services
- Internet
- rent
- utilities
- insurance
- interest
- taxes and licenses

By looking at the expenses of your business and your spending patterns, styles, and tendencies, you can learn where you've made good spending decisions, if you're frivolous (i.e. too much spent on *meals & entertainment* for customers that consistently doesn't yield you much more business), if you're a tightwad (i.e. the amount spent for *repairs & maintenance* is low, but employees keep mentioning "broken" things that need attention), and about many other spending adjustments that might need to be made.

Are there any benefits to examining your spending patterns, styles, and tendencies? Sure. You can learn about yourself as a financial manager of the business so that you can make adjustments that benefit the business. If you've been frivolous, learn to cut back and save the company money. If you've been a tightwad, learn to loosen the purse strings a bit to keep all areas of the business running smoothly. And if you're spending wisely, you can learn from your own good examples of your spending habits and continue the same practice.

Next, using your financial results from your statements, you can create your financial metrics. Discuss with your accountant or business consultant/coach which metrics are most meaningful for your business. The following are a few of the more common ratios.

Return on Investment (ROI)

$$\text{Return on Investment (ROI)} = \frac{\text{Net Profit (net of taxes)}}{\text{Invested Capital}}$$

The Return on Investment ratio (ROI) (or Return on Equity, ROE) measures the rate at which you are making back the money you invested in the business. If your net profit in a given year is $300,000, and you have invested $500,000 in capital, your ROI is .6, or 60 percent. Of course, the higher the number, the better your return.

Gross Profit Ratio

$$\text{Gross Profit Ratio} = \frac{\text{Gross Sales - CGS}}{\text{Gross Sales}} = \frac{\text{"Gross Margin"}}{\text{Gross Sales}}$$

If your business sells "goods," you will have a line item for Cost of Good Sold (CGS) (also known as "Cost of Sales") on your P&L. Gross sales less CGS is also called the "Gross Margin." Gross Margin divided by Gross Sales equals your Gross Profit ratio. For example, if your Gross Sales were $5 million and the CGS was $3 million, your Gross Profit ratio is .4, or 40 percent for that particular time period. Again, the higher the ratio, the better.

Current Ratio

$$\text{Current Ratio} = \frac{\text{Current Assets}}{\text{Current Liabilities}}$$

215

The current ratio measures your business' ability to meet your current cash requirements. Current assets equal the sum of certain assets such as cash, inventory, and accounts receivable that either are cash or will fairly quickly become cash. Current liabilities equal the sum of certain liabilities that will be paid soon, such as accounts payable, taxes payable, payroll payable, and certain loans payable. This ratio should always be greater than 1. For example, if your current assets at a given point in time equal $500K and your current liabilities equal $600K, your Current Ratio is .83. A Current Ratio of *less than 1* means that, if all of your current obligations were due payable today (or next week), you would *not* be able to meet them all. Keep a keen eye on this ratio, or pay someone to watch it for you and report to you regularly.

More ratios to consider, and a brief definition:

- Quick ratio

    The quick ratio is similar to the current ratio, as the current liabilities are used as the denominator, but typically only cash and accounts receivable are used for the assets in the numerator, leaving the inventory valuation out of the calculation. It measures the "quickest" cash available to you.

- Net working-capital ratio

    The net working-capital ratio tells you the amount of liquid capital (current assets less current liabilities) your business uses for daily activities as a proportion of the total assets of your business.

- Profit margin

    Your business' profit margin is the net income divided by total sales. This is a basic ratio that easily tells you what portion of your sales results in profit. You can review the ratio monthly (both for the month only and for year-to-date) to spot seasonal trends.

- Accounts Receivable turnaround ratio
  The accounts receivable turnaround ratio gives you an idea of how well you are collecting from your customers in relation to the increase or decrease in sales in a given month. The monthly sales total is divided by the average accounts receivable for the month.
- Debt-to-Equity ratio
  The debt-to-equity ratio divides your total business debt by the amount of equity on the accounting records. These amounts are found on the balance sheet. If you have business debt, keep an eye on this ratio; you want this number to be low.

Track your business ratios over time. Check how they change from period to period. Compare your results to other businesses in your industry by doing research either online or ask a reference librarian for assistance. If you note these benchmarks that compare your business to standards in your field, it will help you gauge how well you are doing and where you may need to make adjustments.

Review the Financial Present

When a business owner takes a look at what is going on "today" at their business, they're looking at situations and activities they're doing *today* that can help them in the future. What areas can business owners assess presently? The areas include: assessing whether their accounting software is a good choice for them; paying payroll taxes (and any other taxes) on time; when having difficultly paying all bills on time, choosing creditors with whom they can work out a different payment plan; knowing when to get help with the financial aspects of their business (either from their accountant, another outside vendor/financial manager, or from an employee).

What are the benefits of assessing your *current* financial activities? You have more control over the financial side of the business; there is less likelihood that you'll be surprised by a financial-related problem; you're more likely to breathe easier (and sleep better) knowing that your financial issues are reasonably addressed; if you get help with the financial activities of the business from your accountant or financial advisor, you can erase a few items off your "to do" list and have someone handy with whom you can discuss and interpret the data.

Keep current with your financial activities. As mentioned earlier in the story about Jim, if you are a small business owner and do not have the time to take on the financial activities of your business yourself, find someone to do the daily financial work for you. If you do not need someone full time for this duty, either hire a part-time employee or contract out the responsibilities part time. Ask your accountant for advice about how to *separate duties*. This is an important accounting function that protects against the possibility of fraud. (For example, the person who sets up new vendors should be different from the person who processes vendor invoices for payment.)

The person handling the regular accounting functions should perform these duties anywhere from once a week to five days a week. The range depends upon the amount of work the business produces and your business' ability to support the salary or fee of a part-time worker at the current time. Use an accounting software package that is a good match for the size of your business for the next three to five years. (For "smaller" small businesses, packages such as QuickBooks by Intuit or Peachtree Accounting work really well.)

After you or someone else is set up to use the accounting software and is entering the daily transactions of the business, print out reports regularly to keep an eye on outstanding accounts receivable, payables coming due, and your available cash. Review this weekly. Become adept at reading these reports and interpreting them quickly.

More About "Now"

Getting back to Jim's story, if he thought initially that he would pay his payroll taxes on time, I would have suggested that he open a new savings account. Each time he created a payroll check for himself, he would transfer the taxes withheld (and the company contributions toward Medicare and Social Security) into the savings account. That way, the balance of his business checking account would not include those payables. When it came time to pay the taxes, he would transfer the correct amount from the savings account to the checking account, and then make the payment to the government agency.

If doing that was too much for him to handle, he should contact his accountant to take care of it for him. It is worth the expense. Getting penalized by the government for late payments can be much more expensive than paying someone else to handle it on your behalf.

I said it before, and I'll say it again. *Pay your payroll taxes on time!* Even if you are a "solopreneur," do not neglect this payment. Do whatever you have to do to make this payment on time. Many small businesses can pay the federal government their payroll taxes electronically via the Internet. This is a quick and easy way to make the payment. Alternately, have someone else, such as your accountant, make the payment for you. Discuss this option with your accountant. In either case, for monthly payment in the U.S., you have 15 days after the end of a calendar month to make the federal payment. That should be plenty of time to make this payment. Businesses with larger payrolls must pay their withholding tax at the same time as the actual payroll date. If you are in this category, decide if you should have your accountant or payroll service provider handle the tax payment for you.

Are You Having a Little Difficulty Paying Your Bills?

Occasionally, you may find that your business is low on funds. When it comes time to pay, there might not be enough money right now to pay everything that is due. Don't go silent with your creditors. If you need to, contact them to request more time to pay a bill. This goes for the government, too, but I suggest paying all taxes in full on time first. Next, making your payroll and any loan payments due is critical. After that, if you are making payments on equipment that you use to run your business, pay those bills. For the rest, contact the vendor or creditor to discuss stretching out your payment. They would rather hear from you and work out a payment plan that you can handle than:

- Not hear from you at all (i.e., you stop paying on time and they don't know why),
- Hear you make promises to pay that you later cannot fulfill, or
- Receive a check from you that bounces.

A Brief Lesson in Fraud Protection

While writing this book, I came across a true-but-expensive lesson that a colleague, Cindy, experienced in her business. She had a part-time assistant, Kim, whose job, among other tasks, was to write out checks to vendors, which Cindy would sign and mail to pay bills. This arrangement worked well for more than a year. However, through a set of circumstances, Cindy learned that Kim pulled checks from new check stock, wrote herself checks, and then cashed them at a currency exchange.

Kim did this over a six-week period before Cindy found out. Kim was also clever enough to go through Cindy's business mail to pull the bank statement (which Cindy didn't notice because she's very busy, finances aren't really her thing, and she had not been handing over her bank statements to her accountant monthly).

By the time the jig was up, Kim had taken 12 checks, 10 of which she wrote out to herself and cashed, and two of which she wrote to pay for her personal bills.

Kim was prosecuted (her first offense, so she had no previous record that could have been researched before hiring her), Cindy will eventually get most or all of the money returned ($6,000), but the stress of the situation was huge.

So how does a busy entrepreneur protect herself when having others involved in the financial side of the business?

- Put all of your check stock in a safe (this includes both your business and personal check stock).
- Have your assistant line up your bills, and then you write out the checks.
- Ask your accountant for additional ideas on how to protect your assets and not have to do all of the work yourself.

Perhaps your business is in your home and you write all your own checks, so you're thinking you don't need a safe. Really? Do you have teenagers? Do their friends come over to your house? Trust me. Purchase a safe and put your financial instruments into it as soon as possible.

Review the Financial Future

While handling your finances with finesse includes reviewing how the business is doing and comparing that to prior quarters and years, it also involves planning the future. For the immediate future, either learn to create a Cashflow Statement or have your accountant prepare it. Cashflow is very important to small business! For the longer term, you can develop *forecasts*. Your financial skills improve as you learn to forecast future results and plan a budget around it.

As I mentioned earlier in this chapter, the payoff for these financial exercises comes later in the form of increased profit and decreased stress. Stay with me on this one! Setting financial goals for your future is a key financial control for you, both personally and professionally.

In fact, during your fourth quarter, schedule time to forecast the following year. Some accounting software packages allow you to enter a budget or forecast. Otherwise, you can use spreadsheet software (such as Excel or Lotus 1-2-3) to make this task easier.

Cashflow

The Cashflow Statement looks at cash you received and paid out in a certain time period. It may also include the cash you expect the business to receive in a given timeframe (such as a particular month or week) and subtracts the cash you expect the business to pay out in that same time period. For some businesses, they bring in cash at the same time a sale is made. For other businesses, almost all customers set up their own credit terms and pay an invoice after a sale is made (such as 30 days after the date of the invoice). Of course, some customers that have "net 30" terms may pay in 60 or 90 days! Thus, incoming cash is slow.

Hopefully, your cashflow statement shows a positive cashflow!

For the "cash payment" section of the statement, use your expense categories (from the P&L statement) to plug in those amounts. You can use them identically to the expenses in the P&L, or you can summarize several expenses into one category for the Cashflow statement.

Whether you create the Cashflow statement in-house or have your accountant create it for you, prepare it at least monthly (weekly is great, too, since you may pay bills weekly).

Financial Forecast

Your financial forecast takes into account how much money you will need in the future. Because you are a small business owner, do this for your *personal* expenses as well as your *business* expenses.

Personal Expenses

First, review what you will need *personally* as you design your desired lifestyle. Consider the following areas and come up with dollar amounts for each:

- Necessities

  These are the basics: food, home, utilities, repairs, clothing (moderate clothing), medical, automobile, insurance, etc. You may find it easier to estimate this by reviewing several monthly "necessity" expense totals, and then annualizing it. For example, if you look at three month's worth of "necessity" expenses, total those three months together, and then multiply by four to annualize the number.

- Luxuries

  Over your lifetime, the definition of "luxuries" will change. At one point in your life, luxuries may be an exotic vacation, a high-tech TV, or a mink coat. At another point in your life, luxuries may be eating out at a restaurant where entrees cost more than $18, going to the full-price movie theater, and stopping at Starbucks once a week.

  The difference between a median-priced automobile and a luxury automobile would fall into the luxury category.

In any case, decide how much money you want to spend on luxuries over a year's time and plug that number into the "luxuries" category. If it's easier to figure out about how much you want to spend on luxuries every month, multiply that amount by 12 to get your annual amount.

- Between *Necessities* and *Luxuries*

  Most financial people do not look into this category, but I believe that many expenses fall into it. These are things that you really could live without, so they're really not a necessity, but they're not luxuries, either. For example, home improvements (which are more than repairs, as you could live without it, but it would increase the value of your home); a third car for the teenager who just turned 16 (this may become a necessity by the time he or she is 17!); a few fashionable clothing items; a three-day weekend that is a two-hour drive away.

- Taxes

  If your business is a corporation, the business withholds and pays your income taxes, which should take care of most of your tax expense (unless you have personal income from other sources for which you need to pay taxes).

  If you have a sole proprietorship, plan to save between 25 percent to 35 percent of your income (depending on your income level) to pay estimated taxes quarterly.

  If you pay your own real estate taxes on your home, enter that amount into this category.

225

- Paying down your debt
  Do you have school loans? Credit card debt? Any other debt (other than your mortgage and auto listed in the previous categories)? How much do you want to pay on that debt every month? (Multiply that monthly amount by 12.)
- Savings for retirement, college education, etc.
  How much do you want to put away in the next calendar year for special savings? If you're not sure, figure on a monthly amount, and multiply that amount by 12.
- Cash reserves
  How much do you want to have in reserve for the proverbial "rainy day"?

The total of these items is your desired *total gross income* for yourself.

Business Expenses

Second, review what your *business* will need as you design your desired business performance. What dollar amounts will you need for each of the following areas?:
- Your *total gross income* for yourself (just computed)
- Fixed costs
  These are costs that are the same from month-to-month (or quarter-to-quarter). For example, rent, memberships/dues, cell phone (for those who don't call above their limits), insurance, salaries (for non-hourly employees). Project what each fixed cost will be and annualize it.

- Variable costs

   These are all other costs. If you have been in business for at least a year, you can take the last 12 months of variable expenses, and then plan for whatever growth you expect in the coming calendar year by adding a certain percentage to the total. For example, if your variable expenses for the last 12 months were $20,000, and you expect your business to grow next year by 12 percent, next year's forecasted variable costs will be $22,400.

   If your business is fairly new, you may want to consider types of expenses that you anticipate, and then make your best guess regarding what you think your business will need to spend for that type of expense for the next calendar year.

- Taxes

   For "S Corporations," limited liability companies (LLCs), and sole proprietorships, the taxes are paid for in the "personal" finances; "C Corporations" pay taxes on net income (which is after paying you your salary). If your business is outside the U.S., consult with a tax specialist regarding what your business taxes will be over the next year.

- Luxuries

   Same definition as for personal luxuries.

- Extra factors (i.e. "surprises")

   This would be "business surprises" for which you want to have some cash on hand. This is different from "business rainy day" money, as all businesses have small surprises to deal with from time to time.

- Paying down your business debt
  Same definition as for paying down personal debt.
- Cash reserves
  Same definition as for personal cash reserves.

The total of these is your *gross sales target*. On the spreadsheet, you may either list, in detail, all of your forecasted costs (i.e., list each individual fixed cost, variable cost, tax, luxury, etc.), or you may enter one line item for all of your forecasted costs (i.e. one line item for all fixed costs, one line item for all variable costs, etc.). If you are skilled at using spreadsheet software, you can use another sheet in the workbook file to enter the detail, and then pull the subtotals of the detail page onto the main spreadsheet page automatically. Use whichever way works for you (or have someone else create the spreadsheet for you or teach you how to create it using these more advanced features).

Once you assemble these numbers, you can fashion them in the spreadsheet software as your annual forecasts (personal and business). I suggest formatting the spreadsheet in *landscape* so that you can add more columns. While the first column of amounts shown is your *annual* forecast, you can divide that column by 4 to create the next column, which is a *quarterly* forecast. Next, use the rest of the columns to enter your quarterly results. You can also add a column to verify how well you are doing, which you can see at a glance, by calculating the percentage + or − of your *actuals-to-forecast*. With this column you can quickly assess where your business is falling short of the plan and determine how to remedy the situation.

Here is an example of how a portion of your "Business Forecast & Actuals" spreadsheet might look (this example lists details):

| | Forecast | | ----------- Actuals ----------- | | |
	Annually	Quarterly	Quarter 1	% Diff.	Quarter 2
My total gross income	$200,000	$ 50,000	$ 52,000	4.0%	$ 48,000
Rent	64,000	16,000	16,000	0%	16,000
Electricity	1,440	360	375	4.2%	352
Telephone	4,440	1,100	1,020	(7.3%)	1,245
To pay down debt	12,800	3,200	3,600	12.5%	3,200
Cash reserves	20,000	5,000	4,000	(20%)	3,100
Gross Sales Target	$750,000	$187,500	$189,200	0.9%	$181,000

For this type of spreadsheet, a positive percentage is *good* for a few of the line items in the "% Diff." column: the first line item ("My total gross income"), the last line item ("Gross Sales Target"), "To Pay Down Debt," and "Cash Reserves." Since the rest of the line items are expenses, a negative percentage difference is (generally) good because it means you are spending less money (paying yourself is a business expense, but for purposes of reviewing these percentages, it is an exception because it's your personal income). Sometimes less expense also means less sales, which can mean less personal income for you, and that is the only practical downside to lower expenses.

Keep your spreadsheet handy throughout each quarter. Use it regularly to assess where your business is likely to go and how close you will come to achieving your business and personal financial goals.

Financial Discussions with Your Team

In the chapter about leading great teams, we discussed holding regular meetings with various team members. Your monthly meetings are a great time to discuss the company financial results or, if appropriate, a portion of the financial results, such as total sales and certain expenses.

Start by reviewing the previous month's results. If you create your P&L and balance sheet to include a comparison to last year's results at the same time of the year and to include a column for year-to-date, you will have points of reference for your discussion.

In addition, review your cashflow, your forecast-to-actual comparison, and any other pertinent statements.

Make Financial Corrections

Based on your monthly reviews of the financial statements, is there anything that needs correction? Are sales not where they should be, and if so, why? Which expenses look high, and why? What actions can you take to accelerate your cashflow? Would any of the following actions help?
- Increase sales
- Increase prices
- Accelerate your receivables
- Reduce costs
- Slow your payables, within reason

Review Your Pricing Structure

This is also a good time to review your current pricing structure. Is it working well for the business? If so, for how long will it work well? If not, what can be done soon to remediate the issue?

How do you currently set your prices?

- Scientifically: Based on an hourly rate, based on a mathematical formula, or based on market research
- Emotionally: Based on a feeling of what customers will pay

Stories have been told of people selling a product for a particular price, and the product was not selling well. Then they *increased* the price of the product, and they continually sold out. The product didn't change; the perception of the customer changed. At the lower price, the customers believed they were not getting anything valuable. Once the price increased, the customers believed they were really getting something valuable for their money.

"Customers buy results. They don't buy features. They don't buy products or services."

Consider that statement as you revisit your pricing structure.

Debt Reduction

Reducing debt is an important financial area for many businesses. While I do *not* believe that all businesses need to be *debt-free*, I prefer for businesses to not be *debt-strapped*. Business debt can take on several forms, from bank loans and SBA loans to payment plans for equipment or vehicles to credit card debt. The type of debt, the plan to repay it, and the interest paid will tell how easy or difficult the debt is for your business to deal with in the short term and long term.

The Application section at the end of the chapter has several questions for you to consider your business debt and how it affects you and your company.

Cash Reserves

What are "cash reserves"? It is money you set aside for some other use. For example, set aside money as a cash reserve for your business for the following timeframes:

- Short-term: For emergencies, luxuries, etc.
- Mid-term: For capital expenses and growth
- Long-term: For financial independence

With these definitions in hand, you might want to revisit the Forecast spreadsheet and plug in numbers for the cash reserve that more closely represent your plans.

People who don't handle money well or who don't have a plan for their financial future (for the near-term or long-term) set themselves up for pain. Some say "ignorance is bliss," but where money is concerned, ignorance can be like walking around with blinders on each side of your head. By going through the financial steps in this chapter, you can begin to take action on the money you will need to live and prosper for next year and for many years into the future. Having personal and business financial plans can take a load off your mind (and blinders from your head).

Sum it Up

Hopefully you're not too bored with the financial aspect of your business and have learned some tips about how to easily check where your business is "at," how to discover problem areas, and how to plan for your financial future. Apply this to your business by writing out your own plan in your journal and by following the steps in the Application section.

****

You've read through a lot of topics regarding running your business better so that you can catapult your business to new heights of profit. Now comes the *enjoyment* part. The next chapter is the finishing touch as we look at how to design a balanced life.

Application

I have given you a lot of financial work to do in this chapter. While the initial work setting up spreadsheets to calculate ratios, create annual and quarterly forecasts, and prevent fraud is laborious and somewhat stressful, please remember the payoff. These exercises will help you be a better, more informed entrepreneur who can make effective decisions more quickly, thus reducing your stress over the long term.

9.1 How would you describe your spending patterns? As mostly frivolous? As mostly tightwad? Or somewhere in between?

9.2 Why do you think so?

Calculate some ratios! The financial statement you should use to create each ratio shown below is listed.

$$\text{Gross Profit Ratio} = \frac{\text{Gross Sales - Cost of Goods Sold}}{\text{Gross Sales}}$$

9.3 (Calculate the Gross Profit ratio using both last year's P&L statement and your year-to-date P&L statement.)

$$\text{Current Ratio} = \frac{\text{Current Assets}}{\text{Current Liabilities}}$$

9.4 (Calculate the Current Ratio using your current Balance Sheet data.)

$$\text{Net Working Capital Ratio} = \frac{\text{Current Assets - Current Liabilities}}{\text{Total Assets}}$$

9.5 (Calculate the Net Working Capital ratio using your current Balance Sheet data.)

$$\text{Profit Margin} = \frac{\text{Net Income}}{\text{Total Sales}}$$

9.6 (Calculate the Profit Margin using both last year's P&L statement and your year-to-date P&L statement.)

9.7 Which financial ratios are most meaningful for your business?

9.8 What benchmarks exist for your industry's financial ratios?

9.10 What are the trends of your financial metrics?

9.11 How is your business accounting software working for you?

9.12 When will you need a software upgrade?

9.13 Do you need for someone to show you how to use the software so that you're fully utilizing it? (If so, search the Internet for a business that can assist you. At a search engine, type in "get help with _____", and fill in the blank with the name of the software.)

9.14 Have you created a Financial Forecast for your *business* and for you *personally?*

9.15 If so, how does it look?

9.16 How is the forecast working well for you?

9.17 Where does it just not thrill you?

9.18 If not, what is holding you back from getting started?

9.18 What can you do to get started?

9.19 Get a piece of paper or spreadsheet software and start your Personal Forecast. Go back to the pages in this chapter for detailed explanations for each of the categories:

For Personal: Necessities; Luxuries; "Between" Necessities & Luxuries; Taxes; Paying Down Debt; Savings for retirement, college, etc.; Cash Reserves. The total of these equals your Total Gross Income for yourself.

For Business: Your Total Gross Income; Fixed Costs; Variable Costs; Taxes; Luxuries; Extra "surprise" factors; Paying down business debt; Cash Reserves. The total of these equals your Gross Sales Target.

9.20 Have you had an issue with paying your company's payroll taxes on time? If so, what can you do to remember to pay the payroll taxes on time? What would work for you?

• Write it on your schedule (or, add it to your PDA as a "to do" item)

• Sign up for an online "reminder" e-mail service that will e-mail you monthly on the first business day of the month. Here are several reminder services that are all *free*:

 - www.free-minder.com

 - www.latergator.ca

 - www.memotome.com

• If these fail, write a reminder on the palm of your hand in permanent marker!

9.21 What types of debt do you have?

9.22 Do you have normal debt or excessive debt? (Is that debt for your business or for you personally?)

9.23 Do you have debt related to business growth? If so, what is your plan for attaining growth that is directly related to the debt?

9.24 Do you have debt from not being able to delay gratification?

9.25 Do you have a debt repayment plan?

9.26 Do you have an accelerated debt repayment program?

9.27 Based on your responses to the questions above, what do you believe is true about the debt?

9.28 If necessary, what plan will you put in place to deal with it?

9.29 What do you believe can change in the following categories over the next 12 months?
- Change to Sales:

- Change to Spending:

- Change to the Pricing Structure:

- Change to Business Debt:

- Change to Cash Reserves:

Design a Balanced Life

*"The Entrepreneurial Dream: A business you
enjoy that produces plenty of money.
Time to spend on activities and with
people you love. A balanced life!"*

—Glory Borgeson

Susan owns a temporary employment agency in a southwestern state and employs five office staff people full time. In addition, her company has between 250 and 350 temporary employees working at client sites at any given time. As she built the business in its early days, she worked between 60 and 80 hours a week. Over time, that schedule took its toll on her personal life and her health. Her husband and kids learned to "get by" without her; however, increased misunderstandings, temper flare-ups, and hurt feelings put a wedge in their relationships. Susan began "eating on the run," had no time for exercise, and began to gain weight. She also got sick more often than she used to.

When Susan realized one June day that she felt run down (and had felt this way for about two months), being the wise woman she is, she made an appointment with her doctor for a physical. She found that her blood pressure was on the high side, but it was at the borderline point between taking medication to lower it or using diet and exercise to naturally lower it. She decided to change her life and opted for the diet and exercise method in order to avoid medication.

The first thing Susan did was take a long, hard look at her business. She worked on creating a vision for what she wanted for her business and for her personal life, and then put together a strategy to implement it. She knew she needed more help in her office in order to bring her workload to a more manageable level and in order to grow the business. (She only had one employee at this time who handled paperwork in the office.) She had no business debt, but had been in business for four years already, and so she decided to talk to her banker about getting a loan to help jump-start her new plan.

She needed two additional people as soon as possible, and one more in about six months. Between them they would handle sales, recruiting, and maintaining employee relations with the temporary staff. Susan identified that her sales people would need to have skills and personality similar to hers, while the others needed skills appropriate to the tasks of employee relations for a temporary work force outsourced to clients.

Next, Susan planned for her "team creation" and listed the people with whom she already did business, such as her insurance agent, accountant, banker, attorney, and graphic designer. She also knew that when she added new full-time staff she would need to provide technology and communications tools, and set out to ask other business people who they used locally to provide this service. In addition, she decided that she should also start to inquire about public relations experts. Susan made a plan to contact her existing experts to meet with them and tell them of her ideas to change the business and to ask for their advice, as she would need to update her insurance, check on any legal updates in her field, consider updating her marketing materials, and streamline accounting operations while strengthening her business against possible fraud.

Since she planned to hire new people, Susan put together some sales training materials from sales training companies for classes she found helpful in the past, and contacted those organizations for their schedules for the coming 12 months.

After discussing her health issues and plans for change with her husband, they decided they should work together to figure out their personal financial goals. Since it was June, they decided to plan for the next six months, and to revisit their numbers in October for how well they had "guessed," and then to plan for the following calendar year. After figuring out their personal financial goal, and subtracting her husband's income, the net result was the financial goal for her business to provide for her income. Then Susan took a look at her business financial statements for the prior year, and for January through May of the current year. She started with those amounts and increased them for her plan to bring on new people, increase her sales, and increase the money paid to the higher number of temporary employees. This gave her a better idea of her goals on paper.

The initial work to create a plan and start to put it in place took time and energy. However, Susan knew what the payoff would be. She knew that two or three months of contacting certain people, securing funds, hiring new employees, training them, and the paperwork included for all of it would keep her work hours at about the same level for a while. She just kept the goal in sight and remembered the vision she developed of changing her business and her life. Susan's vision kept her motivated.

After her initial hard work, it began to give her the results she hoped for. Susan hired sales people who had her skills and personality and an additional employee to handle most of the temporary employees' issues. She worked with her own "team of experts" on an advisory basis to streamline certain operations to ensure that the business would not fall apart if she took a day off. She also found she had time to join a local business group to meet other entrepreneurs in order to share information and gather nuggets of wisdom from their expertise.

Susan now had a growing business, trained people to run more aspects of it, and she was able to reduce her work week to 40 to 50 hours. She also was able take a day off once in a while, go to her kids' events, and take a family vacation. Susan also joined a health club that was open early and closed late, put a larger refrigerator in her office, and ate more fresh fruit and vegetables. Her weight went back to normal, and so did her blood pressure.

The four months it took to change her business and her life was well worth the effort. Yes, it was hard work and the planning and implementation was "extra" work, in addition to what she already had on her plate. But Susan kept her vision in mind and strove to reach her goals. Her business grew in volume and in net profit, and she was able to lower the amount of time she spent both in and on the business.

Susan could truly say that she increased her profit and decreased her stress, catapulting the business to a new level of profit!

What About You?

By now, with all of the work you have done while reading this book, you have a design that will help you increase the profitability of your business while also reducing your level of stress. It might still be in the form of many notes, either in your journal or in the Application sections, but you are well on your way to getting those notes into a plan that turns into action. Your plan will give you energy that is both mental and physical. The success of your business plus the feeling of more energy may even add years to your life. Let's review a few topics that will help you turn your notes into action.

Restate Your Vision

Take a moment to restate your vision for your business and for your personal life. Write it in your journal in summary fashion. In your vision, what are you doing? How is your business different from what it is today? How is your personal life different from what it is today?

Set Priorities

While reading this book, you have taken a lot of notes and made some commitments. Take some time to review and prioritize all the things you want to do. Besides business issues, additional priorities could be in the areas of family, finances, relationships, physical, intellectual, and spiritual. Highlight your to-do list items by marking them in some way (i.e. use a highlighter or use a pen and put a star next to the items, etc.). Then transfer those items onto another sheet (or to spreadsheet software, which is recommended since you will sort these items). In your list, what items do you want to accomplish in the next month? In the next three months? six months? nine months? 12 months? Mark those items accordingly. If you used spreadsheet software for this exercise, you can easily sort those items. Then you will see which tasks you want to accomplish soon, sorted together, and which will either take longer to finish or that can be started later.

Plan Well in Advance

Use whatever scheduling or journaling plan works for you in order to plan daily, weekly, monthly, quarterly, annually, and a few years out. Plan your focus days, buffer days, and free days. Plan to take training and leadership development seminars for yourself. Plan for the priorities you just identified and noted.

Control Your Time

Focus on sticking to your plans. Use the delegation/duplication discussed in an earlier chapter to help you achieve your goals regarding time. Go back over your notes to review how you are going to delegate tasks and/or duplicate yourself.

Less Stress = Less Stuff

Do you have clutter in your office space? Use the methods discussed in chapter 3 to clear out clutter. Get help if you need it to keep *stuff* from becoming a stressor.

Remove Whatever Gets in Your Way

What are you tolerating in your business and in your personal life? If and when situations get in your way, if you can responsibly, ethically, and legally remove them, do so. This will clear the way for less stress and more success.

A Well-Balanced Life

We all desire a well-balanced life. For many of us, choosing to own a business was part of that plan. Being an entrepreneur presents its own challenges and stresses, though. A life that is well-balanced includes a balance in areas such as work (*enjoyable* work!), family, friends, exercise, rest, spiritual renewal, community participation, and recreation. Entrepreneurs often find themselves out of balance in several of these areas and with increased stress.

The American Institute of Stress reports that over 60 percent of peoples' visits to their doctor are for symptoms that are stress-induced. Stress increases our likelihood to have a disease or to experience injury.

We business owners often think if we spend more and more time on our business we will be more successful. However, there is an *opportunity cost* associated with this line of thinking. Once we get to a certain point, the rewards go down as our stress level increases.

Truly, if we take some time away from our business to rejuvenate, our business will benefit because we will be more creative and productive.

When I was in coaching school, I learned that there are four basic outcomes of coaching:
- Awareness
- Purpose
- Competence
- Well-being

Being "out" of any of these areas can increase our stress level. When stress is high, it's time to take a break to answer a basic question for several areas of our lives:

What's important? (for each of the following areas):

- My business
- My commitments made to others
- My health
- My relationships

In earlier chapters, we discussed many ways to change your business so that your stress level is reduced. Once those are in place and you have more time to destress, you will have more opportunity for destressing activities.

Destress

Think about the activities that you find enjoyable and that help lower your stress level. Think of 10 activities and list them in your journal.

Of the 10 activities you listed, put a star to the left of three to five that work best for you at alleviating stress. These are your "*Key Relaxation Activities.*" Write next to those activities about how long it takes to do that activity, including driving time.

How can you begin scheduling one of your *Key Relaxation Activities* each week? Will you put it into your schedule?

Exercise

At minimum, try *walking* in 15-minute increments. If you try to do this every day, you will at least have exercised for 15 minutes each day. Keep up a good pace when you walk.

If possible, join a health club that is open for extended hours and has equipment and facilities you enjoy (for example, if you really enjoy swimming, make sure the facility has an indoor pool). Don't join any fitness classes that have a set schedule; that would add too much stress to your life.

Breathing Exercises

Simple breathing exercises are a great way to decrease your stress. You can do this at home, at your office, or any place where you are waiting for a minute or two.

While sitting in a comfortable chair:
- Inhale for a count of four,
- Hold your breath for a count of four,
- Exhale for a count of four,
- and hold your breath (out) for a count of four.

Repeat four more times, for a total of five rounds. Really fill up your lungs on the inhale. Close your eyes for this exercise to maximize the effects of the relaxation.

Nutrition

Sometimes I think people are going to cry when I mention that good nutrition will help to lower their stress. (*But fast food is so easy!* Yes, and it also keeps you unhealthy!) When you are unhealthy, you cannot handle very much stress! Here are some simple goals to help you feed your body with energy:
- Increase your fresh fruit intake, especially in the morning, to four to five servings.
- Choose whole grain breads that are not baked with hydrogenated oils

- Increase your fresh vegetable intake, especially at lunch and dinner.
- Bring fruit and cut-up vegetables with you during the day for snacks.
- Drink plenty of clean water.

Doing the steps listed above will automatically help you lower the amount of processed foods and sweets eaten.

Decrease Drama

Do you sense a lot of drama in your life? Drama certainly leads to increased stress. Ask yourself the following questions:

- What drama in your life is the result of outside influences?
- Which of those are brought on by circumstances?
- Which of those are brought on by other people?
- What drama in your life do you bring on to yourself?
- What can you do to decrease the drama in your life?

Reflect on the questions, and your responses to them, in order to reduce the negative effect that drama has on your life.

To Sum Up Destressors

Get enough sleep, strive to eat a healthy diet, fit exercise into your schedule, and try to schedule one of your *Key Relaxation Activities* weekly. And remember to keep your free days as truly *free*.

It's Your Life

There are still a few questions for you to ponder in the Application section. Go through it and make notes, also using your journal for more writing space.

Designing a balanced life is about creating the business and life you want. It allows you to define your business, take into account who you are and how you work, and it allows you to make adjustments as circumstances change.

> Your Business: *Increased Profit*
> Your Life: *Decreased Stress*

That is my goal for this book: To instill in you the ability to design the business you want so that you also get the life you want. Whether your business is rather large or quite small, I believe you can achieve it if you set your attention and intention to increasing profit and decreasing stress. Then you will see your business catapulted to new heights of success!

Application

Now and Then

10.1 During the last year, what have you enjoyed doing for fun? Take a few minutes to list below whatever you recall.

10.2 What did you enjoy doing when you were a child (say, between the ages of 3 and 12)? What summer activities? What winter activities? What outdoor or indoor activities? Take a few minutes to jot down whatever comes to mind.

10.3 What was it about your childhood activities you just wrote down that was wonderful?

10.4 What is the difference between what you did for fun in the last year and what you did for fun as a child?

10.5 Usually, it is the activities we did for fun as a child that bring us the most enjoyment and lower our stress levels. As you look at your childhood activities, what can you reasonably do today as an adult to bring back that level of enjoyment?

Final Application Notes

You have already completed a lot as you worked through this book!

Schedule some time to go through your notes. Categorize them as needed wherever topics fit together.

What are your priorities that will help you to increase profit and decrease stress:

10.6 In the next 2 weeks?

10.7 In the next month?

10.8 In the next 6 months?

10.9 In the next year?

10.10 What plan do you have in place to accomplish your goals?

10.11 How are you going to control your time?

10.12 What have you already done to remove clutter and stuff from your business and your home?

10.13 What else still needs to be done?

10.14 How are you going to get it done?

10.15 What has gotten in your way of catapulting your business to new heights (without piling a lot of stress on yourself at the same time)?

10.16 Do you think that something can be done about it?

10.17 What can you start to do in the next month?

10.18 How are you doing in terms of your health and fitness?

10.19 What will you do to make health and fitness a priority?

10.20 What creative ideas can you come up with in order to make this fun and something you will continue to do?

Final Thoughts & a FREE Offer

*C*ongratulations! *"Catapult Your Business to New Heights"* is no ordinary book and I've encouraged you to do a lot of work while reading it. Your thinking, pondering, sorting, writing, rewriting, planning, and strategizing for your business has been an accomplishment in itself.

My hope is that you have culled some nuggets of wisdom that, together, form a plan for your business and your life that is achievable beyond your dreams!

Would you like to explore further how you can specifically apply the principles of this book to your own business?

I'm offering a **free coaching session** to *Catapult* readers. Together, we can assess your business needs and determine how you can get your business to the next level, create more profit, and do it with less stress!

Contact me by e-mail at the address below to schedule your free coaching session so that we can discuss how to *catapult your business to new heights of profit.*

Gratefully,

Glory Borgeson, president
Borgeson Consulting, Inc.
Glory.Borgeson@BorgesonConsulting.com
www.GloryBorgeson.com

About the Author

Glory Borgeson is a business coach, author, and speaker, focusing on helping entrepreneurs reach new levels of profit and success, while at the same time maintaining a healthy, balanced lifestyle. She has over 25 years' experience in many different industries, including oil & gas, waste/environmental, airlines, manufacturing/ERP, supply management, utilities, and various types of small businesses.

Glory speaks and writes about a variety of topics of interest to small business owners and to executives in the first two years of a new position. Visit her website at **www.GloryBorgeson.com** for current information regarding recent articles, speaking topics, and coaching programs available.